Arthur Penn's *Bonnie and Clyde*

Few films in the history of American cinema caused more intense critical discussion and greater emotional debate than Arthur Penn's *Bonnie and Clyde*. This provocative portrayal of Depression-era life on the run, delivered with visual panache and a hip sensibility, ushered in what came to be categorized as "the New American Cinema." Focusing on a story set in the 1930s, yet clearly fashioned to resonate with the countercultural tenor of the 1960s, the film remains compelling for today's viewers by virtue of its central love story and inevitable tragedy, its subversive statement and its sympathetic connection to the communal impulse. This volume includes freshly commissioned essays by leading scholars of Arthur Penn's work, as well as contributions from Penn himself and scriptwriter David Newman. They analyze the cultural history, technical brilliance, visual strategies, and violent imagery that marked *Bonnie and Clyde* as a significant turning point in American cinema.

Lester D. Friedman teaches humanities at the SUNY Health Science Center and film at Syracuse University. He writes about multicultural issues, medical humanities, British film and culture, and American cinema.

CAMBRIDGE FILM HANDBOOKS SERIES

General Editor
Andrew Horton, University of Oklahoma, Normal

Each CAMBRIDGE FILM HANDBOOK contains essays by leading film scholars and critics that focus on a single film from a variety of theoretical, critical, and contextual perspectives. This "prism" approach is designed to give students and general readers valuable background and insight into the cinematic, artistic, cultural, and sociopolitical importance of selected films. It is also intended to help readers grasp the nature of critical and theoretical discourse on cinema as an art form, a visual medium, and a cultural project. Filmographies and select bibliographies are included to aid readers in their own exploration of the film under consideration.

Arthur Penn's
Bonnie and Clyde

Edited by

LESTER D. FRIEDMAN
Syracuse University

CAMBRIDGE
UNIVERSITY PRESS

PUBLISHED BY THE PRESS SYNDICATE OF THE UNIVERSITY OF CAMBRIDGE
The Pitt Building, Trumpington Street, Cambridge, United Kingdom

CAMBRIDGE UNIVERSITY PRESS
The Edinburgh Building, Cambridge CB2 2RU, UK   http://www.cup.cam.ac.uk
40 West 20th Street, New York, NY 10011-4211, USA   http://www.cup.org
10 Stamford Road, Oakleigh, Melbourne 3166, Australia
Ruiz de Alarcón 13, 28014 Madrid, Spain

First published 2000

Printed in the United States of America

Typeface Stone Serif 10/14 pt.   *System* DeskTopPro$_{/UX}$ [BV]

A catalog record for this book is available from the British Library.

Library of Congress Cataloging in Publication data
Arthur Penn's *Bonnie and Clyde* / edited by Lester D. Friedman.
p.   cm. – (Cambridge film handbooks series)
Filmography: p.
Includes bibliographical references and index.
ISBN 0-521-59295-X – ISBN 0-521-59697-1 (pbk.)
1. Bonnie and Clyde (Motion picture)   I. Friedman, Lester D.
II. Series.
PN1997.B6797   1999
791.43'72 – dc21   98-32173
                                   CIP

ISBN 0 521 59295 X hardback
ISBN 0 521 59697 1 paperback

For Rae-Ellen
Who Brought Back the Light

Contents

Contributors

Matthew Bernstein (Emory University) teaches film studies and directs the graduate program at Emory University. He is the author of *Walter Wanger: Hollywood Independent* and the coeditor of *Visions of the East: Orientalism in Film*. His reviews and articles have appeared in a variety of books and journals, including *Wide Angle* and *Film Quarterly*. With the urban historian Dana White, he is currently researching a history of moviegoing across the color line in Atlanta.

Steven Alan Carr (Indiana University and Purdue University at Fort Wayne) teaches courses in film, mass media, and interactive multimedia. His book *The Hollywood Question*, which explores the accusation of Jewish control over Hollywood, is forthcoming from Cambridge University Press. His article on *The Smothers Brothers Comedy Hour* won first place in the 1991 Society for Cinema Studies essay contest and was subsequently published in *Cinema Journal*.

Diane Carson (St. Louis Community College at Meramec) teaches film studies/production and is coeditor of two recent anthologies, *Shared Differences: Multicultural Media and*

Practical Pedagogy and *Multiple Voices in Feminist Film Criticism*. She worked on the award-winning documentary *Remembering Bonnie and Clyde* (1994). Her other areas of interest include the pedagogy of film instruction and the development of Asian studies curriculum.

Lester D. Friedman (SUNY, Health Science Center and Syracuse University) teaches medical humanities, multiculturalism, British cinema, and American narrative film. His most recent books include *American-Jewish Directors* (coauthor), *Fires Were Started: British Film and Thatcher*, and *Unspeakable Images: Ethnicity and American Film*. Currently, he is completing a book on Steven Spielberg.

Liora Moriel (University of Maryland) is a graduate student. Since the original release of *Bonnie and Clyde*, she has been a feminist and lesbian activist in Israel, as well as a world-traveling photojournalist, singer-songwriter, and teacher. Two of her songs are featured in David Sigal's short film *Conception*.

David Newman (scriptwriter) started his professional career at *Esquire* magazine (where he co-created the "Dubious Achievement Awards") and went on to a distinguished career as a writer for theater productions and films. He has been nominated for the Academy Award and won the New York Film Critics Award, the National Society of Film Critics Award, and three Writers Guild of America awards for various screenplays (several coauthored with Robert Benton, several with Leslie Newman, and several that he wrote solo). In addition to the one he wrote for *Bonnie and Clyde*, his scripts include *What's Up Doc?*, *Bad Company*, and *Superman, the Movie*.

Arthur Penn (director) began his career in live television and eventually directed shows for *The Colgate Comedy Hour*, *The Philco-Goodyear Playhouse*, and *Playhouse 90*. Penn has directed both Broadway shows and Hollywood films, and his illustrious career has spanned four decades (see Filmography). He also created the Actors' Studio Free Theater in New York City, an organization devoted to presenting plays out of the commercial mainstream, and currently serves as its director.

Stephen Prince (Virginia Polytechnic Institute and State University) has written *Movies and Meanings: An Introduction to Film* and *Sam Peckinpah's The Wild Bunch*; he is also the editor of *Visions of Empire: Political Imagery in Contemporary American Film* and *The Warrior's Camera: The Cinema of Akira Kurosawa*. Currently he serves as book editor for *Cinema Quarterly*.

Acknowledgments

The oft-quoted cliché reminds us that "success has many parents, but failure is an orphan." So it is with this anthology. Over the time that it has taken me to assemble this volume, I have been blessed with the good fortune to work with a roster of generous and talented contributors from various academic institutions. Several have collaborated with me previously, and I take their willingness to do so again as a high compliment; others are sharing their thoughts and energy with me for the first time on this project. All have functioned far beyond the expected professional parameters, and their enthusiastic exchange of ideas with each other has turned this book into a truly collaborative experience. To all of you, I express my thanks for your professional patience, your personal kindness, and your individual perseverance.

In addition to the work of these colleagues, this book is graced by the articles written by Arthur Penn and David Newman. Both men deserve our gratitude. Many of the writers in this collection called upon either Arthur or David (and sometimes upon both) to answer a specific question, to verify a particular fact, or just to listen to their ideas. While certainly not agreeing with all that they heard, both men generously gave of their time and even allowed contributors to view valuable documents. Their input has certainly made this book more definitive, not to mention far more enjoyable, than it would have been without their assistance.

I would also like to thank Dede Allen for graciously providing me with pictures for inclusion in this volume. The people at Jerry Ohlinger's Movie Store in New York City were also very helpful in providing necessary stills.

In Syracuse, I am supported, as always, by a wonderful array of colleagues and friends. At the SUNY Health Science Center, my department chairperson, Margaret Braungart, did everything possible to provide me with the time and resources necessary for completing this project. My secretary, Sharon Osika-Michaels, made my life immeasurably easier with her ability to get all the things done when I needed them. At Syracuse University, Owen Shapiro continued to function as a sympathetic listener, supportive counselor, and good friend. My research associate at the E. S. Bird Library, Denise Stevens, saved me countless hours by answering all my questions and gathering whatever documents I required.

This is my first book with Cambridge University Press, and it has been a joy to work with the people there. Beatrice Rehl, the fine arts editor, initiated and supported this volume, providing excellent advice and wise counsel. I was honored to be one of the "boys." Anne Sanow took over the project at a formative stage and oversaw its journey with determination and tact. Susan Greenberg edited these essays with a keen eye and insightful alterations. Andy Horton, general editor of the Cambridge Film Handbooks Series, has been instrumental in getting the project through the various stages in the publishing process. Thanks to all for your hard work, jovial companionship, and professional guidance.

My children, Rachel Elizabeth and Marc Ian Friedman, have heard enough about *Bonnie and Clyde* to last them a lifetime – maybe two lifetimes. Yet I have certainly benefited from their humor and prodding during this book's gestation. My parents, as always, have given me love and affection.

To Rae-Ellen Kavey, I owe a debt far beyond words. Her compassion and kindness, spirit and intelligence, make all things possible.

LESTER D. FRIEDMAN

Introduction
ARTHUR PENN'S ENDURING GANGSTERS

HISTORICAL PERSPECTIVES: COUNTERCULTURAL CINEMA

Boy meets girl in small-town Texas. Their crime spree begins as girl goads boy into robbing a grocery store; they speed out of town in a stolen car, spirits high. Against the backdrop of Depression-era America, this attractive and stylish young couple and their accomplices career through stickups and shootouts, kidnappings and narrow escapes, ultimately meeting their dramatic end in a legendary ambush. Based on a true-life story, few films in the history of the American cinema have inspired more critical discussion and greater scholarly debate than has director Arthur Penn's *Bonnie and Clyde* (1967). Along with *The Graduate* (1967) and *Easy Rider* (1969), Penn's provocative evocation of Depression-era life on the run, delivered with visual panache and a hip sensibility, ushered in what came to be categorized as "the New American Cinema." Such an artistic renaissance, as several writers in this anthology detail, resulted from a unique nexus of conditions within the American film industry and the society that surrounded it: the economic breakdown of the Hollywood studio system, the ideological move toward more explicit depic-

I

tions of sex and violence, the historical impact of escalating the Vietnam War, the aesthetic influence of European art house films, and the cultural creation of a new film ratings system. Ultimately, according to Glenn Man, these three films "reassessed the American cinema's achievement, deconstructed and restructured its traditional forms, and exploded or questioned its dominant myths."[1]

From our current historical vantage, it seems easy to understand why these three watershed films captured the spirit of a turbulent America in the late 1960s and early 1970s. It was an era lacerated by cultural divisions that grew wider and deeper in a jagged trajectory from the Woodstock Nation to the Weathermen, from the Chicago riots to the My Lai massacre. Although none of these films directly confronted the social and political issues gnawing at society's most sacred institutions, each encapsulated part of the zeitgeist spawned by the passionate clash of cultural beliefs. So, for example, *The Graduate* exemplified the emerging generation's fear and loathing of their parents' plastic existence, scornfully depicting an older social order devoid of personal and professional values. *Easy Rider* offered sixties moviegoers a countercultural alternative: a liberating life on the road heightened by the mental and physical stimulations of sex, drugs, and rock and roll. Both films reflected a youth culture profoundly anxious about its future and self-consciously preoccupied with its present.

Yet it is *Bonnie and Clyde*, the film formally set in the past rather than in the present, that most poignantly evoked the contemporary exuberance, the complexity, and ultimately, the sadness of those times. The film's screenwriters, David Newman and Robert Benton, clearly fashioned their engaging outlaws to resonate with the countercultural sensibility of the 1960s. As Newman notes in his article written for this book:

> It is about people whose style set them apart from their time and place so that they seemed odd and aberrant to the general run of society. Most importantly, they did this by choice. . . .

. . . What we were talking about was what is now known as "the Sixties." . . . If the film is "really about" something, it is about that most of all.

For the new heroes of the youthful culture that burst into prominence during this time, acting "odd and aberrant to the general run of society" was precisely the goal. They expressed their joy and discontent in a kaleidoscopic, magical mystery tour of long hair, drugs, war protests, psychedelic music, bell-bottoms, flower power, free love, and social causes. To them, the anarchic Bonnie and Clyde became historical counterparts to their own personal and communal struggles: a young and attractive couple fighting against the restrictive moral codes and hostile social institutions of their time.

But beyond the film's importance in cinematic history, the events surrounding the release of and public response to *Bonnie and Clyde*, more than for almost any other American film, is a story in which the offscreen activities are as important as the onscreen performances. *Bonnie and Clyde* reflected and influenced a critical time in American life. The film stood at a profoundly significant cultural crossroads: a point where American values veered from a comfortable fifties' mentality to a more complicated reconfiguration of the world; where the old Hollywood system cracked under the impact of new ideas and technologies; where the center of film criticism shifted from the stodgy Bosley Crowther to the pugnacious Pauline Kael; where fashion designers emulated Hollywood instead of Paris; where visual styles incorporated European aesthetics; where film became as intellectually legitimate as literature and painting; where sex and violence replaced romance and innuendo; where revolutionary political fervor overcame moderate activism; where a youthful film audience took possession of America's sensibilities. All this is important for understanding the context that generated the film as well as the central role that the film played in bringing these conflicts and transformations into clear focus.

The appeal of *Bonnie and Clyde* for its late-sixties audiences seems clear: it fired a subversive shot across the prow of mainstream American society. By doing so, the film forced an older generation of moviemakers, critics, and audiences – one shaped by their Great Depression and World War II experiences – to confront the emerging power and rebellious values of a new and different generation – one molded by the assassination of John F. Kennedy and by the Vietnam War. Yet such a moment, although important as the cultural context of the film, is inherently fleeting: its very currency assures its transience. After all, if *Bonnie and Clyde* only reflects those heady days of the 1960s, however effectively it captures their style and spirit, it can be dismissed as merely a nostalgic relic for aging baby boomers or historical artifact for enthusiastic film scholars. It therefore seems reasonable, particularly in an anthology geared to current film students, to explore the sustaining pleasures this film offers for viewers in the late 1990s.

CONTEMPORARY CONNECTIONS: EPIPHANIES AND EPITHETS

We might ask the following question: in a world characterized far more by button-down shirts than bell-bottom jeans, where global-warming seminars engage far fewer passions than did Vietnam sit-ins, does this once-revolutionary film still exert an intellectual and visceral hold on contemporary audiences? Surely its violence, which alternately scandalized and titillated earlier viewers, no longer causes the same degree of moral outrage or agitated shock when juxtaposed against the blood-soaked frames in the latest Oliver Stone, Quentin Tarantino, or Martin Scorsese feature film. Indeed, when *Bonnie and Clyde* airs on commercial television, it now runs unedited and rated as PG, the once-controversial death sequence posing few problems for vigilant censors.

Yet even with the vast changes in tastes and mores, *Bonnie and Clyde* remains as compelling for viewers today as it was for audiences in 1967 for three basic reasons: (1) the emotional resonance of the central love story; (2) the sympathetic connection to the communal impulse; and (3) the intellectual fascination with inevitable tragedy. Ironically, then, it is not so much the film's glitz and glamour, nor even its visual audacity, that allows *Bonnie and Clyde* to transcend its time period, although such elements certainly contribute to its lasting popularity. Rather, it is the viewer's fundamental response to Bonnie and Clyde, not as generational symbols or historical icons but as fated individuals struggling for personal and communal connection, that remains essential to the film's continuing appeal.

Tales of lovers doomed to disaster rest at the heart of many enduring works of literature and film: Oedipus and Jocasta, Othello and Desdemona, Heathcliff and Catherine, Rhett and Scarlet, Rick and Ilsa. These couples, among many others, form the spiritual lineage of the emotionally crippled Bonnie and Clyde; like their fictional ancestors, the brash yet vulnerable Clyde and the brazen yet fearful Bonnie strike a responsive chord that connects them to a modern generation searching for its own pathways to each other and to the disquieting world that surrounds them. The nuanced characters created by director Arthur Penn and the scriptwriters David Newman and Robert Benton embody an almost universal yearning for intimate communion: flawed people desperately striving, often unconsciously and extemporaneously, to transform their best individual impulses into a bond, no matter how fleeting and temporary, with others.

Take the scene in which a distraught Bonnie abruptly abandons the gang, after the carefree joyride with Eugene and Velma ends with Bonnie's icy premonition of death. When a distraught Clyde finally catches a glimpse of her in the distance, he sprints across the desiccated cornfield, an ominous shadow sweeping darkly with him and blackening the sunny landscape. He clasps her in his arms, touches her hair, and gently caresses her face. "Please, honey," he begs, "don't ever leave me without saying nothin'." Far more than their words, the emotions etched in their haunted faces express the inextricable bond between these restless, fumbling characters. From this time forth, and at whatever cost to their individual psyches, Bonnie and Clyde no longer function as separate entities. We instinctively grasp that their need for each other transcends personal eccentricities, individual failures and particular weaknesses. It is a moment of sheer and total connection with the audience, a frozen second of unmitigated acceptance and unspoken understanding – an emotional epiphany for both characters and viewers.

For Clyde, this fundamental drive for human connection leads to the construction of an extended community or, perhaps configured more accurately, an alternative family. His need for a communal sanctuary differs markedly from Bonnie's desire for a more restrictive relationship. The addition of C. W. Moss, along with Buck and Blanche, moves Clyde beyond the role of male companion and into that of surrogate father. One could easily assign archetypal family roles to the entire Barrow gang: C. W. as the slightly slow younger brother; Buck as the backslapping big brother; Blanche as the prim older sister. In this scenario, Bonnie fulfills the most complex role. Within some scenes, she is the harsh stepmother, alternately ridiculing Blanche, rebuking Buck, and chastising C. W. Other times, she seems far more maternal: sensitively comforting a grieving Blanche, humorously playing with Buck, or playfully cajoling C. W. The point, however, is not to assign rigid roles to each character; rather, it is to understand that Clyde's impulse to surround himself with a "family," one connected more by attitude than by blood, reflects his overwhelming desire to establish a secure place for himself surrounded by those who truly care about him.

Finally, let me turn to the inevitability of Bonnie and Clyde's destruction, a narrative structure as ancient as the Greek tragedies of Sophocles, Aeschylus, and Euripides. We quickly sense that however much the characters of Bonnie and Clyde might attract us on a variety of levels, their path will almost certainly lead to their deaths. Within the narrative itself, Bonnie eventually accepts that death remains the only possible conclusion to their story; fleeting respites filled with mundane communal activities provide only illusionary glimpses of temporary normalcy. The film's outcome, therefore, is never in doubt. As a result, we tend to concentrate on what these characters choose to do with their allotted time, on how they utilize the modicum of free will left for them to exercise.

Such structural considerations force us to examine how the violence in *Bonnie and Clyde* inherently differs from the casual carnage omnipresent in contemporary movies. Put simply, Penn uses violence as a morally justified conclusion to the actions that precede it. His films have none of the ritualistic sadism of Scorsese's *Goodfellas* and *Casino*, the playful amorality of Tarantino's *Reservoir Dogs* and *Pulp Fiction*, or the gratuitous bloodletting of Stone's *Natural Born Killers*. For Penn, violent action may be an understandable response to events, it may even eliminate a persistent problem or help attain a desired goal, but he never absolves whoever employs it from moral responsibility. More importantly, once violence has been used (or even threatened), it sets in motion an unstoppable series of events that trap the participants in a web of their own creation.

Great works of art stand the test of time because they simultaneously reflect the period of their creation and transcend it. Such fluidity inspires each generation to discover meanings significant to them within the lines of an epic poem, the frames of a silent movie, or the bars of a musical composition. More than thirty years after its initial release, we can affirm *Bonnie and Clyde*'s status as landmark in the history of American cinema. It clearly marked a turning point in American film history, as movies made under the once powerful studio system gave way to more independent, experimental, and youth-oriented films. Yet to approach this film as merely the hoary relic of a bygone age is to ignore its enduring power. One of the few films that force viewers to meditate seriously upon how violence, both on the screen and off, shapes our lives, it also speaks to the profound yearning for human connection that permeates our daily existence. Thus *Bonnie and Clyde* remains a vital and engaging movie that intellectually challenges and emotionally touches contemporary audiences. I have little doubt that it will continue to strike a responsive chord in those who watch movies in the new century and beyond.

THE BOOK: CREATORS, COMMENTATORS, AND CRITICS

The essays in this anthology represent a wide spectrum of critical methodologies, ideological perspectives, and personal responses to *Bonnie and Clyde*. As such, they testify to the film's continued ability to inspire a broad range of opinions and to maintain its emotional sway over modern viewers. My introduction establishes the movie's significance for viewers in the late sixties and its relevance to contemporary audiences. In the articles that follow, the director Arthur Penn and the screenwriter David Newman discuss their personal involvement in the film's creation.

Penn's essay outlines how he came to direct *Bonnie and Clyde*, his state of mind prior to the film's production, his feelings about the Hollywood studio system, and the various obstacles he faced during and after the shooting and editing of the film. It is a fascinating look from the inside out, a rare glimpse into the collaborative process from the point of view of the man who stood at the center of this creative enterprise. David Newman's piece, also written expressly for this book, is a witty discussion of the various interpretations of the movie visited upon him by critics and commentators over the last three decades, including several by other contributors to this volume. In his essay, he details what he and co-writer Robert Benton thought their screenplay was about at the time they wrote it and over the subsequent years.

The book's focus on technical and thematic aspects of *Bonnie and Clyde,* on the film's cultural and critical receptions, and on its significance as part of American culture follow these comments by two of its creators. These begin with two articles about history: one about documented events, the other the evolution of ideas. Diane Carson's exhaustive history of the incidents surrounding the actual Bonnie and Clyde provides rare eyewitness accounts of the outlaws' exploits. Moving beyond the strictly factual, Carson speculates on the nature and function of myth and legend in our culture, demonstrating how Hollywood re-packages infamous personas for consumer consumption. Focus-ing on 1967, the year that *Bonnie and Clyde* was released, Steven Alan Carr paints a portrait of an America at war with itself over cultural values and government policies. Such a piece allows the reader to understand why this film resonated with viewers living in those turbulent times.

Matthew Bernstein's essay examines the visual style of *Bonnie and Clyde*. He explores, in concrete detail, the distinctive look and feel of the film, examining the visual and editing techniques that captured the attention of viewers and critics. Here readers learn about the technical aspects that make the film such a unique creation.

The following essay by Stephen Prince zeros in on the most controversial aspect of *Bonnie and Clyde*: its violence. In addition to noting Penn's artistic influences, Prince situates the film's violence within those debates about the social effects of mass media that erupted in the late 1960s and continue today. Read-ers are then invited to compare *Bonnie and Clyde* with several contemporary movies.

In her piece, Liora Moriel offers a "queer" reading of this film. Bringing a fresh theoretical approach to her analysis, she focuses on queer theory as a tool for uncovering hidden meanings. Such a contemporary vision allows readers to see *Bonnie and Clyde* through one current perspective and to understand how the film remains receptive to diverse readings.

Finally, this book includes two widely divergent responses to *Bonnie and Clyde* from 1967. Bosley Crowther's scathing attack in the *New York Times* aptly demonstrates the vitriolic negative response the film engendered from many mainstream reviewers. It also marked Crowther's last conservative volley, as he was perceived to be clearly out of touch with contemporary sensibil-ities and was relieved of his preeminent position at the newspaper. Conversely, Pauline Kael's passionate defense of the film in *The New Yorker* marked her ascendancy as the most powerful movie critic in the United States. Together these reviews allow readers to comprehend the firestorm of controversy ignited by the release of *Bonnie and Clyde,* one pitting old aesthetic values against new ones and establishing a dividing line between a generation of directors, moviegoers, and critics.

NOTES

1. Glenn Man, *Radical Visions: American Film Renaissance, 1967–1976* (Westport, CT: Greenwood Press, 1994), 1.

Making Waves
THE DIRECTING OF *BONNIE AND CLYDE*

The script for *Bonnie and Clyde* entered and exited my life a few years before it eventually became a film. I recall that it was some time in the early sixties. At that moment it appeared to me to be a good gangster film, but I decided that a gangster film was not where my interest really lay. Frankly, I wasn't at all certain I wanted to make another Hollywood film. I will explain my ambivalence shortly, when I write about *The Chase*. And, if I were to do another film, I felt it should be a story with a broader social theme than a flick about two thirties bank robbers whose pictures I remembered as a couple of self-publicizing hoods holding guns, plastered across the front page of the *Daily News*.

François Truffaut had read the script, and then Jean-Luc Godard. Robert Benton and David Newman know why those matches never resulted in a film. They did say something to the effect that Godard wanted to shoot it in three weeks in the middle of a Texas winter, which somehow didn't please them. They wrote splendidly of the travails of getting a fine script made into a film in an introductory essay to *The Bonnie and Clyde Book*, aptly titled "Lightning in a Bottle."

A couple of years went by, and Warren Beatty approached me

with the script. He now owned an option on it. We had made a film together called *Mickey One*, and our friendship had endured that. Now, Warren wanted us to make *Bonnie and Clyde* and thought Clyde a fine role for him. Despite Warren's passion for the film, I again declined it because I could not see making a gangster film, despite the very good script. But I did want to make another film with Beatty.

Warren grew tired of my indecision and took advantage of the presence in New York of the head of the William Morris Agency, Abe Lastfogel. We were both clients of that agency then. Warren flew in, and the three of us lunched at Dinty Moore's. I didn't stand a chance. Warren can be the most relentlessly persuasive person I know, and when he joined forces with Abe Lastfogel, a true elder statesman of the motion picture business, I had capitulated by the time Warren had finished his complicated order for a salad. Abe explained that Warren and I could have a sizable amount of autonomy and the privilege of "final cut." That meant a great deal to me since I had had two dreadful experiences where my films were edited by someone else, without even consulting with me. That proved persuasive.

So, I was going to make a film called *Bonnie and Clyde*!

Where was I in my life, and why had I allowed a couple of years to elapse since I had made a film?

My recent experience with a big film had left me depleted of enthusiasm for films made in the bosom of Hollywood. It was titled *The Chase* and had a script authored in large part by Lillian Hellman from a play by Horton Foote. It was produced by Sam Spiegel, who was returning to Hollywood with the triumphs of *Bridge on the River Kwai* and *Lawrence of Arabia* wreathing his head like olive crowns. They were excellent films, and Spiegel deserved credit for inducing David Lean to direct them.

Spiegel had left Hollywood years before as something of a figure of mirth under the name S. P. Eagle, which he employed to disguise his Middle European origins. He was notorious, as I was later told, for giving huge New Year's Eve parties that were clearly beyond his means. Now he was returning to Filmland a heroic figure. In Europe, Sam had made his fortune. The fact is that Sam was an educated and very intelligent man who was enormously wealthy from those two great films; now, he was a successful producer and large stockholder in Columbia Pictures and wanted to make a film in Hollywood with the biggest names he could gather. And he did. Brando, Redford, Jane Fonda, Robert Duvall, Angie Dickinson, and many other highly esteemed actors were in the cast. I had directed a play of Lillian Hellman's on Broadway, *Toys in the Attic*, which won the New York Drama Critics Circle prize. Lillian urged Sam to hire me. After a meeting between us, he agreed and I was delighted with the opportunity.

I had made three films by that time, but my reputation rested on the more secure grounds of five Broadway hits. Among the three films, only *The Miracle Worker* was what might be called a success. The third film, *Mickey One* starring Warren Beatty, was still being edited. Spiegel did not get to see it until we were well under way and deep in preparation for *The Chase*. It was a film I had made for Columbia under an arrangement that followed *The Miracle Worker* in which I could make any film I wanted provided it cost no more than a million dollars and was not "dirty." In exchange for the paltry budget, Columbia (whoever that was) was not permitted to read the script. When Columbia and Sam had finally seen the film, I was about to start photography on *The Chase*. A conference call from the executives and Sam came through to my office on the set that I would characterize as "clenched teeth, pseudoenthusiastic." It was clear they had hated *Mickey One* but feared upsetting me on the eve of the start of their great and certain megahit film.

Lillian and I worked on the screenplay for *The Chase* in New York while Sam was negotiating the deals for the major roles in Hollywood. He would consult with us about the actors and often suggest that we come to Los Angeles where we would all be able to confer face-to-face on casting, script, and staff. Lillian was reluctant to return to Hollywood, which had thrust her aside for her political persuasions. I was perfectly happy to delay departure from my family, my wife and two young children, for as long as I could. But Sam eventually prevailed, and we moved our work to California.

What neither Lillian nor I knew then was that Sam, in addition to having Hellman write the screenplay, had simultaneously employed another screenwriter to adapt the Horton Foote play. Hollywood has its evil ways, and contempt for "the writer" probably heads its dubious list. So you hire another "writer" to cover the first.

While we were having great success in attracting splendid actors to the piece, Lillian was experiencing an increasing dysfunction in finishing the script. Her health was not good, and her cigarette consumption reached Olympic gold medal numbers. I was frankly delighted when she went off to Palm Springs but dismayed when the flow of pages trickled to an occasional one or two and then none. She was distressed with me because of the pressure she felt I was exerting; and I was. Sam was displeased with the progress of the script and brought in Horton Foote to "just touch up the dialect."

In fact, Horton wrote a sizable portion of the end of the film. Of course, Lillian resented Horton's work on the script and my complicity with Horton and Sam. Horton and I had worked together a number of times in live TV. Lillian was furious and scornful of Horton's southernisms. He had written a line of dialogue that contained the phrase "chopping cotton."

"Who ever heard people talk of 'chopping cotton,' " Lillian exclaimed. "They pick it, not chop it." Horton was a southerner and knew whereof he spoke. Lillian, although born in New Orleans, had spent little time in the South, where they do speak of "chopping cotton." In fact, they chop and pick, two different functions.

I was in a place that causes me distress to write of, even now. We were in that terrible Hollywood game of preference and rejection. I was forming new alliances and allowing older ones to be compromised, all in the expedience of rushing to commence the film on the chosen date. Hellman was in physical distress. Her cough grew worse and resounded from her desert balcony. Her symptoms accumulated, and she became less able even to converse about the film script. She left California with the script unfinished and with considerable anger toward Sam, Hollywood, me, and all concerned.

Foote finished the script, and we began shooting the film. Actually, and quite amazingly, it proved to be a good script. However, during the shooting, occasional, odd pages would come down to the set from Sam's office. Bizarre, small changes in language, which quite distressed me, were introduced. Perhaps they were chosen by Sam from the other script, which I never saw, by the other screenwriter. Perhaps Sam "wrote" them himself. In any event, the movie bears all the signs of a true Hollywood industrial production. No real authorship, only an accumulation of minor inspirations. It was bewildering.

Somehow a pretty good film emerged. The best part of the experience was working with the extraordinary actors who brought invention, enthusiasm, and high spirits to the project. Brando was a delight. He would improvise after having rendered a take that was word perfect. And the improvisations were often brilliant. Sadly, very few remain in the finished film.

Yet, I never felt it was my film. My discomfort grew daily. My stomach sent messages that it was having serious difficulty digesting the daily diet of ignominy I was feeding it. I failed to take the film under my control. Sam was the éminence grise whose figure as a Hollywood titan hovered over everything. I should have confronted him and claimed control of the film or relinquished it totally. I did neither. I continued to deceive myself that this was Hollywood and many fine films had been made that way. That was true, but they were made by directors who were much more adroit at managing the system than I was.

Sam slept late in the morning and then would call me on the set to find out if everything was going as scheduled. They were tedious and patronizing phone conversations. One day, as I hung up, I realized Brando had been watching me. With his unerring eye for psychological gestures, he approached me. By now we had become good friends and enjoyed a lot of laughter. As he came closer, I saw that his shoulders were raised and his hands out in helpless surrender. He fixed me with his devilish grin. "It's me," I said.

It was. I was getting beat up on that film and allowing it to happen. The director of photography, an old Hollywood hand named Joseph LaShelle, was determined that he was going to light the picture so as to bring wonder and amazement to the eye. Night after night we sat, this magnificent cast and I, while he lit and lit and filled the dark with brilliance and then stopped the lens down to where he felt he had sculptured the night. The cast and I were by that time weary and our inspiration sorely diminished. "It's all yours," he would say. By then it was often one o'clock in the morning.

The shooting ended, amazingly enough, on schedule. Now, we were going to edit it into a motion picture. With the exception of my first movie, also made in Hollywood, I had controlled the editing of my next two, *The Miracle Worker* and *Mickey One*. Editing is a phase of filmmaking I deeply enjoy. So many rhythmic choices can be invented that energize a film and give surprise, alternation of expectation, and the pleasure of the deep richness of actors' performances. The nuances and often "inappropriate behavior" that fine actors bring to their art are discovered, uncovered, and made vivid by their placement in the film's emerging life. It's a thrilling alchemy; hard work, but often editing discovers gold. I looked forward to making *The Chase* into a film.

Sam and I had discussed where I would edit. We had agreed upon New York, because I was contracted to direct a play on Broadway after the completion of shooting. Shortly after I returned to New York I had a call from Sam. "Where do you want to edit the film, Hollywood or London?" he asked, as if we had never decided on New York. Of course, he wanted control of the editing, and it was done in London against my protests. It is moderately well edited, although its pace is stolid and far too "significant." The greatest loss the film suffered in editing was that some of Brando's extraordinary improvisatory work never survived Sam's orthodoxy and his implied authorship. All the actors in that remarkable cast had done fine work. The pity is that not enough of it is left there to be seen in the edited film.

The film opened to a response that was certainly less favorable than we might have wished for. I was sick of movie shenanigans and mostly sick of myself for abdicating responsibility and not having the sense to reach a contract on each point with Spiegel.

Brando's imitation of me was true to the end.

The play I directed, *Wait Until Dark* by Frederick Knott, was a sizable hit on Broadway, and for the second time in my life I said to myself, "To hell with Hollywood; I can live happily doing plays." I withdrew from films and for the next couple of years declined to consider some wonderful scripts that were offered me. When they were made into movies, they proved to have been fine indeed. I envied the directors who had made them.

Teaching is not a particular passion of mine, but it was something I did occasionally enjoy. The dean of the School of Art and Architecture at Yale, whom I had met at a discussion I took part in at Yale, persuaded me to teach a postgraduate course to six people, each of whom had already made a film. I met the students, and they were bright and seemed pleased at the prospect of working with me. We started, and one day a week I would drive to New Haven, teach, and drive back to New York. It was arduous but damned nourishing, and it did wonders for my psyche and stomach, which clearly were closely in touch with each other. Slowly I was developing an appetite for the fray of wrenching a movie out of the chaos of my gut. Just after I finished the year's teaching, Warren Beatty called with *Bonnie and Clyde*.

I recount all of this to explain my ambivalence toward committing to the film. I was still gun-shy, and it took a friend like Warren to persist and refuse to accept my skittishness. Warren is one of very few people on whom, in hard times, one can really count. Ten years later, when help was needed by my daughter who was ill and stranded on an island off the coast of North Africa, Warren went immediately to work to get a Columbia Pictures corporate plane to pick her up. Fortunately, she was able to get on a commercial flight out and return to the States to be treated for her bout with hepatitis. But Warren would have succeeded in a few hours, and he would have helped us inestimably. Lillian Hellman, who shared my warm opinion of Warren, dubbed him "the best foul-weather friend" one could have. True.

Now I was about to start a new film with that friend. But what film? At our house in the country, where I usually retreat to work, I knew after several readings there was something about it bothering me. Robert Benton and David Newman, fine writers, had taken from the little biographical material available, the presumption that there was a sexual triangulation with Bonnie, Clyde, and the character C. W. Moss (eventually played by Michael J. Pollard). Incidentally, C. W. Moss is an amalgamation of several characters who joined and left the Barrow gang. That sexual ménage à trois struck me as both too sophisticated and, even if true, divergent from the direction I felt the film should go. My recall from early memories was that the crop of bank robbers and eventual "Public Enemies," so designated by J. Edgar Hoover's expanding FBI, were in fact country folk; they were farmers or children of farmers, bumpkins most of them, frequently all but illiterate. They were willing to settle for the small sums they snatched from country banks, but they certainly did not seem to me figures that belonged in complicated sexual arrangements.

Recently published books about the FBI confirm that Hoover, superb Washingtonian that he was, spent large sums and made multiple appearances before congressional committees, elevating these country bank robbers into a national menace. "Public Enemy" numbers 1, 2, 3, 4, etc. were all out in the middle of the country. By Mr. Hoover's lights, nothing was going on in the large cities that merited placing urban dwellers on his "Public

Enemy" list. Luciano, Lansky, Madden just didn't rate "Public Enemy" status by Mr. Hoover's estimate. And "G-men" against "Public Enemies" provided the perfect scenario for the enlargement of his fledgling criminal agency into the FBI, a *federal police force*, where none had existed previously. With great information-gathering forces at his capricious disposal, J. Edgar maintained, for the rest of his days, that there was no mob, no Cosa Nostra, no crime families, only "Communists" and his chosen "Public Enemies."

Laws were changed, and the FBI was empowered to extend its might beyond state limits in their relentless pursuit of these "merciless criminals." J. Edgar Hoover utilized his powers to assemble a vast body of information about everyone whose acquiescence he would need to increase his puissance. The list covered congressmen, future presidents, and justices, as well as numerous celebrities. He blackmailed the nation for at least three decades. The Cold War gave him an even greater opportunity to practice his brand of "Americanism." He skipped around the maypole of "Americanism" with Joe McCarthy, Roy Cohn, and Richard Nixon, chanting ditties of patriotism for the nation they held in thrall.

The Great Depression formed itself as the banks and financial institutions pursued a positively Dickensian value system. They persisted in the punitive posture of moneylenders, Scroogian to the core. "If you can't pay back the money and interest, then we will foreclose and take possession of the equity against which we lent you the money" – very simple economic behavior. Punishment must be meted out to the delinquent. Breadlines formed, bonus marches took place, the capitalist premises of the nation were in disarray. The problem was that after the farms had been taken by the banks and left fallow, the banks found themselves equally fallow. They failed. A huge number of unworked farms can hardly be considered assets. The displaced farm families were cast off to seek a livelihood anyway they might. Resentment against the Establishment and its economic bastions burst out. It was only a small step for the dislodged farmers and their children to pick up some of the plentiful weapons and turn them against the repositories where they believed the money was.

It was from this admittedly simplistic perspective that I began to see the film. Naive and living on poor emotional rations was the way I described the characters. Benton and Newman agreed that the sexual sophistication in the original script did not contribute to the film we now wanted to make. We talked and moved in the direction of a simpler tale, one of narcissism, of bravura, and, at least from Clyde's point of view, of sexual timidity. Our talks were wonderfully funny and pointed. They gave me even greater confidence and enthusiasm for the film. As a kid in the Great Depression, I had developed a certain sympathy for the people I saw resisting the circumstances that prevailed in the country. Our divorced family was poor, quite poor. There was to my youthful perception a sense that what we observed of our American life was *unfair*. "Ah, America," my mother, who had come here as a teenage girl, would lament in disappointment at the hard times we were living through. Yet there was plentiful evidence that not everybody suffered in the Depression. The rich practiced their mores and lived by values that bewildered us. Debutantes, speakeasies, mobsters, and high society filled the pages of the tabloids.

We had the tone of the film. It was to start as a jaunty little spree in crime, then suddenly turn serious, and finally arrive at a point that was irreversible. How would the characters perceive their lives? Bonnie had her "poem." It was epitaphic and romantic, and more than slightly self-aggrandizing. I had Bonnie's version of their death, but not a true closure to the film. How to end it?

There was an accurate historical representation in the script of the death of Bonnie and Clyde. Yet the ending troubled me. Written in the script, as it apparently happened, the police officers fired relentlessly into Bonnie and Clyde. There were eighty-seven bullet hits on their bodies. I wanted something different to close this film. The words I employed to myself and later to

Warren were "spastic, yet balletic." You can imagine the quizzical responses that awkward description brought.

In a minor epiphany I saw the ending – literally saw it as it
emerged in the final film. Certainly the slowed motion of Akira
Kurosawa's great films inspired me. Although I did experiment
very briefly in my first film, *The Left-Handed Gun*, with film speed
changes, their true use was not clear to me until I saw Kurosawa's
Seven Samurai. His sweeping, slow-motion sword fights were
thrilling. But I wanted something that contradicted the subtle
beauty of slow motion. I felt it should act against itself so that a
terrible tension occurred. That became the ending. It brought
delight and horror. The horror was more potent for the *New York
Times*'s film critic than the delight and formed the keystone of
his assault on the film.

Warren was concerned with another area of the script. As it
had been reconstructed with the deletion of the ménage à trois,
the result was that no completed sexual event between Bonnie
and Clyde occurred. Only a few failed attempts. That seemed all
right to me. Because I was so concerned with keeping an abiding
naïveté in the story I thought, when Bonnie published the poem
about them, that would suffice as gratification.

Beatty thought not. He felt that Bonnie and Clyde should
finally make love. I resisted that for a while. I was satisfied that
Benton and Newman and I had found an adequate substitute for
the ménage à trois. But I suspect I didn't have a clear enough
vision of the romance that the story would generate. I finally
agreed rather churlishly. Warren was right. It proved a vital in-
gredient.

In Pauline Kael's lengthy and sometimes insightful essay from
The New Yorker magazine (included in this book), she may have
succeeded in communicating the impression that this film came
into existence despite my efforts. I believe she managed to speak
with Warren Beatty and Bob Towne, both of whom live in California. I live a few blocks from *The New Yorker* offices in New
York City. She never made any effort to contact me or to inquire

about certain assumptions she made concerning scenes and viewpoints expressed in the film.

I will now engage in a Kael-like presumption. She was so militantly opposed to the theory of the auteur that had been advanced by Truffaut and others in the *Cahiers du Cinéma* and embraced by some fine American critics, that she went to considerable lengths to disengage the director from the *Bonnie and Clyde* film. Determined to oppose Andrew Sarris and other critics who espoused the auteur theory, she suggests an image of filmmaking that permits movies to come into existence despite the interference, she seems to imply, that is the principal contribution of directors she does not admire. That is her privilege, but she apparently was not in the market for any facts that might contradict her view.

She then breaks the news to us that I am neither Fellini nor Bergman. That came as a terrible shock to me. Here all along, I thought I was both.

"Where shall we put the camera? How do we want to approach this scene, funny or startling or a combination of both? How will we photograph it? Where will the camera be? How do we rig it to accomplish that? How should it look? What are they going to wear in this scene? I know, guys, let's take a vote!!"

Kael may not think highly of me, but if she thinks that *Bonnie and Clyde* is "art," I can tell her it didn't get to be that through democratic process. If I am not its "auteur," whatever that is, I sure as hell directed *Bonnie and Clyde*.

Back to what actually took place. Bob Towne, a close friend of Warren's and soon to become one of mine, was now helping us with the screenplay. His was a new eye and a needed one. In the few contemplative moments Towne and I had, we became aware something was awry in the middle of the story. A reunion scene with Bonnie's family was always in the film script. Bonnie's desire to see her mother and sister seemed a proper turn. But her longing for her family emerged from her general sense of disaffection for the changed circumstances with Clyde. Her displeasure with Blanche's presence in the gang, Buck's ridiculing her attempt to write poetry, and the absence of sexual contact with Clyde produced an increasing malaise in her. But the family reunion remained simply another event in the journey toward their end.

To describe how that was enhanced and made memorable, I will remind you of a different, fine section of the film.

The Barrow gang needs a car. Their stolen car has torn its oil pan in a getaway from a brazen bank robbery. While Velma and Eugene (Evans Evans and Gene Wilder) are necking on a porch, we see, in the background, the theft of Eugene's car. Eugene and Velma give indignant chase, then suddenly, they themselves become the objects of a chase by the Barrow gang and are captured. After they are forced into their stolen car, now the property of the Barrow gang, they become quite friendly with all of the gang. Buck tells his "don't sell that cow" joke, Velma's true age is revealed to Eugene's chagrin, and they share hamburgers and much merriment until Bonnie asks Eugene what he does for a living. He responds, "I'm an undertaker." A dark adumbration sweeps across Bonnie's face. She turns to Clyde and says, "Get them out of here." Eugene and Velma are abandoned at the side of the road. The gang speeds off.

In the original script this sequence took place as a comic moment, I believe, after Bonnie had visited with her family. The scene with her family originally was almost without dialogue. Towne and I sensed vaguely a problem we felt existed, but change in the scenario is very hard to introduce as a film sweeps toward shooting. The desire for order, any order in the chaos, is passionate.

I came back home to New York for a last family visit before photography was to commence and brought the script with me for Peggy, my wife, to read. She had on previous readings been somewhat uncertain about it. Peggy is a family therapist. Now she read the script and, without my raising the question of the family reunion scene, unerringly pointed to the Eugene and Velma scene. "That has to precede the family reunion," she said. Her reasoning was absolutely clear. Bonnie's need for her family of origin was not because of a general discontent with the immediate circumstances of the gang and her forced sexual abstinence. She needed her family because death, Eugene's being an undertaker, had forced itself into her consciousness.

Clearly the line of the film would have a much stronger thrust with that change. I returned to Los Angeles and talked with Towne. He agreed. He went off and wrote a scene in which Clyde, playing the great protector of Bonnie, tells her mother that he'll look after Bonnie and as soon as they have enough money, they will move just down the road from her mother. "You do that, and you won't live long," Bonnie's mother responds. Bonnie is struck dumb, and we see her panic. She turns toward Clyde; he is silent and chastened. Their future has been spoken.

I realize I am describing what seems to be an orderly process. That is never the case once a film starts tumbling toward photography. Every phase of the movie demands attention simultaneously: casting, clothes, art direction, where to shoot it, who is going to play Bonnie, what photographic style? In no particular order, a thousand chaotic questions occur all at once. That's movies!

The filming began in Texas. We journeyed out each day to another of the small towns that Bob Benton so recalled from his youth. We were most fortunate in having chosen Dean Tavoularis to design the film. He came highly recommended by Bob Jiras, who would be in charge of makeup. And the clothes, by Theodora Van Runkle, fit the image of the movie exquisitely. The "look" of the film became famous. It reminds me of some events that connected most amusingly.

Just before we were going to begin photography, the head of production at Warner Brothers asked Warren and me if we wanted to shoot the film in black and white. We gave the suggestion some brief thought, but we were certain that we wanted to avoid the pseudodocumentary tonality that black-and-white photography would have implied. We knew we were making a film for "now," not a remake of "then." After the film came

FIGURES 1 and 2
Evolving dramatic structure: the placing of the "car stealing" scene before the "family reunion" scene dramatically shows Bonnie's conscious understanding that she and Clyde will die violently.

out and enjoyed broad acclaim, the great Swedish director Ingmar Bergman was asked his opinion of the film. He spoke very flatteringly of it and of me. Then he added, "The only thing I would have done differently is shoot it in black and white."

The cast of *Bonnie and Clyde* consists of some of the finest actors of our time. Only nine principals, but what a nine! Beatty, Dunaway, Gene Hackman, Estelle Parsons, Michael J. Pollard, Denver Pyle, Dub Taylor, Evans Evans, and, in his first film, Gene Wilder.

The shooting of the film is not an experience I recall clearly, and I am not going to attempt to recount the incidents I do remember. They are typical of most movies and are about as amusing as someone forgetting to put film in a hand-held camera. Indeed, one day the camera operator and I were tied to the front of the car, standing on the old bumper. Clyde drove at high speed, and we photographed the gang fleeing the Joplin shootout. We shot them head-on. We returned to base and then discovered there had been no film in the Arri. Impossible to happen with a professional and experienced film crew? It did. We lived through it.

The film was almost finished. Jack Warner, the surviving Warner Brothers brother, had been in New York almost all the while the film was planned and shot. He was selling the studio! He returned to Hollywood just as we were finishing the last automobile "driving shots," which were done with rear projection. We had been in Texas for almost all the filming. Now we were on the "lot" for just a few days of rear projection.

The first day Jack Warner returned from selling the studio, Walter MacEwan, still the head of production, came to our set and called Warren and me to one side. He told us that the "old man" was back, and he was worried because Jack seemed depressed. He was going to have lunch in his private dining room, and there was "nobody" to sit at the table with him. Walter meant no producers, stars, or directors were around. The only other feature film shooting at that time was *Camelot*, and Joshua Logan and Richard Harris didn't want to come to lunch. They were having some trying times. The great Warner Brothers lot was a pretty barren place.

Warren and I knocked off shooting for an extended lunch break and went to the dining room. It was just us and a few Warner Brothers executives. Jack told some raunchy jokes, and there was appropriate laughter, mostly from the executives. Warren kept teasing Jack by trying to get him to tell us to whom he had sold the studio. Jack evaded any response until Warren told him that he knew who the new owner was.

"No you don't," Jack said.

Warren said something like "look at the water tower. Whose initials do you think those are?" Warren was pointing to the huge WB logo that adorned the tower. Jack was puzzled and then realized what Warren meant. WB as in Warren Beatty.

"Get outa here, you snotty kid," Jack growled at him, even as he laughed heartily. "The Colonel," as he was called, was his old jovial, bawdy self. Lunch over, Warren and I went back to work.

Jack was a charming tyrant and in his day was a much feared character. All those "Major Studio Buccaneers" were despots, with some justification. Studios were tough places to run, particularly in the days when they were turning out a movie a week. For years they made about fifty movies annually. Schedules and budgets were sacred. Jack Warner was notorious for arriving on a set where a film was running over schedule. He would say to cast, crew, and director, "You finish this Friday!" The protestations made no difference to Jack Warner; the picture finished that Friday. "But we haven't shot . . ." "Never mind, you finish Friday." And they did!

We were in our last day of shooting the final automobile interiors, and, it being Friday and our wrap day, we scheduled a traditional wrap party for that evening. That is a final get-together of cast and crew with some drinks and a buffet meal and a lot of self-congratulation. We were pleased with ourselves. We were right on schedule. We finished the automobile stuff, and the movie was "in the can." The only thing remaining to be done was to take the still photos of Faye and Warren that would be part of the opening titles of the film. We were going to do that on Monday in a still-photo studio, with just makeup and a wardrobe person. The crew would be off the picture and off salary.

Jack arrived at our wrap party. He had heard about the photos on Monday. "You wrap the movie tonight," he said. It was so bizarre a remark that we thought he was kidding. Not at all. This was a last hurrah. "You wrap the movie tonight." We pointed out that that meant the entire crew would still be on the clock, to be paid while they ate and drank. "You wrap the movie tonight!" Walter MacEwan stood behind Jack with a chagrined expression, as if to say, "What can I do?"

That's what we did. It was beyond reason. We took the stills! The cost was preposterous. The movie was wrapped on that note of mordant tantrum.

I went to work on the editing with Dede Allen in New York. Dede is a superb film editor, and we worked together for the first time on *Bonnie and Clyde*. It was a partnership that endured for a number of years and quite a few films.

At a certain point, near the end of the editing, we brought the film to Hollywood, where the final "release prints" were to be made. We were required to show the film to the studio for them to plan distribution and marketing. It was shown to the head of Warner Brothers distribution, Ben Kalmenson, who promptly pronounced his infallible judgment, "It's a piece of shit."

That judgment brought little pleasure to our hearts. Bob Towne, to whom we also showed the film, emerged from one of the small projection rooms on the Warner lot and declared that the film "would do thirty million." Warren and I didn't believe him either.

Walter MacEwan, an excellent gentleman, suggested that we show the film at the Colonel's house – the title his executives addressed Jack Warner by. His now former employees acknowledged that the Colonel was suffering a sense of loss at having sold the studio. We would take the film to Jack's house and show it in his elegant projection room. They thought doing that, as they had done so often in the past, would cheer the Colonel. His small staff and Warren and I were to be the audience with him. We arrived with the film. The Colonel warned us, "If I have to get up and pee during this, you'll know the movie stinks."

A few minor courtesies were exchanged, and the projection started. We were still in the first of the ten reels that constituted the movie when Jack arose and left the room. We looked at each other, uncertain whether or not to stop the projection. We didn't. The film ran on. Jack returned to his seat. The film narrative began to gain velocity, and we thought we had him. No. He was up again, peed, returned, watched, peed, returned, peed, and the longest, most diuretic film in human memory, came to an end.

Silence.

"What the hell was that?" spake the Colonel.

Silence.

Nervous small talk.

". . . the hell was that?" he said again.

Warren Beatty rose and began to speak about the great gangster films that Warner Brothers had been famous for through several decades. Finally, he concluded, "So you see, Jack, this is, in a sense, an *homage* to those great films."

Silence.

". . . the fuck is an *homage*?"

There was a burst of explanations, everyone defining it differently but always with the emphasis on the "great old Warner Brothers gangster films." Finally, Jack broke into his smile and nodded. The sentence had been passed. The Colonel approved . . . after a fashion. In fact, he had already decided to bury the film with poor bookings and a minimal advertising campaign. But for the instant there was general relief and a rush to an adjoining room for refreshments. For some reason, Jack and I remained behind in the projection room.

It was not a conventional projection room. Besides a Renoir and a Monet on one wall, the other walls were bookshelves that contained, bound in gray green leather, the scripts of all the films ever made by Warner Brothers. Hundreds of script binders, leather bound, beautifully maintained, graced the walls.

Here were Jack and I left in each other's uncomfortable presence. I had made this painful film, and he was no longer in charge of his studio. What to talk about?

"Tell me, Jack, of all of these films, which one are you most proud of making?"

I expected he would say *Casablanca* or one of the great Cagney gangster films. Or maybe one of the terrible World War II films he had the studio make. He had been a colonel during the war and was fiercely proud of his rank.

"You're from the fucking theater, right?" He knew that I had done a number of plays on Broadway.

"I'll tell you what I'm most proud of, . . . the son of a bitch." And he walked directly to one of the walls and pressed apart two binders and extracted a small pamphlet.

"Here's what I'm most . . . The fucking theater . . . When we started, we were making these little pictures, see, and everybody wanted to get hold of some of the plays that had been around on Broadway, but the sons of bitches wouldn't sell us. They didn't want pictures made of their art. No, we were too goddam . . . I got down on my . . . Begged! And finally the son of a bitch sold them to me. Me, me before the other guys . . . Fucking theater snobs! Belasco! That piece of . . ."

And he thrust the pamphlet at me. It was a list of the plays David Belasco had produced and directed and controlled as one of the dominant Broadway entrepreneurs of an earlier day. *Girl of the Golden West* was one of the titles that I remember. There were titles of perhaps a dozen plays, none of them a conspicuously great work of art. Nevertheless, they had represented legitimacy to Warner and the other film pioneers. And to have acquired them was for him his greatest triumph.

So what do I think now?

Well, the film is over thirty years old. There has been a beautiful new print struck, and the sound has been remastered. A copy of the movie resides in the Library of Congress. When a film endures as *Bonnie and Clyde* has, there is an air of mystery about it. Why? It had its moment in the times we were living in. But why still now? I have no explanation.

It's a good film. It is a damned good film. I'm proud and surprised I made it.

DAVID NEWMAN

What's It Really All About?

PICTURES AT AN EXECUTION

In September 1996, two debuts occurred simultaneously: the premiere of the digitally restored print of *Bonnie and
Clyde* and the unveiling of "the world's largest screen" at Radio
City Music Hall in New York. Arthur Penn and I, as well as our
wives and friends, had been invited to this grand event; we sat
in the first row of the mezzanine like crowned heads in the royal
box. (The fact that the friends included a few movie stars didn't
hurt.) After marveling at the quality of the restored film – nuances of color never seen in the original and mumbled ad-libs
from the extras in the Okie camp sequence never before heard
suddenly manifested themselves – I found myself delighted that
our movie, which once shocked "the fabric of our society," was
now playing in this bastion of "family entertainment." It
seemed absolutely right to me, because, in fact, one of the things
the film is "about" is family.

My coauthor, Robert Benton, and I used to call it "the creation
of the artificial family," and it is a theme that has run through
much of our subsequent work, whether in collaboration or apart.
In essence, the idea is that people from fractured or nonfunc-
tional biological families find themselves reaching out to strang-
ers to form tight little units to replace what's been missing.

32

That's just one of the things the movie was "about," to us, but over the past three decades (and in this book, as well), you will see that a lot of folks have their own theories as to "what it really means."

After the screening, we all went to a nearby restaurant for a late dinner and congratulatory drink (we all still thought it was a pretty swell movie we'd made). Although I'd seen it countless times, I'd noticed only that night an image that struck me as intentional. Benton and I had written in the screenplay that, shortly before the finale, one lens of Clyde's sunglasses pops out of its frame. (There's even some dialogue about it: Bonnie says, "You gonna wear 'em like that?" and Clyde answers, "Drive with one eye closed.") Well, that night I suddenly spotted that, in the penultimate shootout in which Buck is killed, the remaining members of the gang make their getaway in a car with one headlight shot out. It may not be a big deal to anyone, but to me it clearly presaged the doom to come, and when I mentioned it to Arthur, he grinned and said, "I'm glad you finally noticed."

That put me in mind of an article written by a woman in an obscure film journal about two years after the picture had opened and was becoming the subject of learned dissertations. I don't recall her name or the publication, but the piece she sent us was about "the symbolism of broken glass in *Bonnie and Clyde*." At first we all thought that it was a great hoot, since as far as we knew there was no such symbolism. Yes, there was a lot of broken glass. Some of it was carefully written in the script, and some was added by Arthur during the shoot because, as he said, "glass breaking is fun to see on screen." I had begun to read this "insight" with a smirk plastered in place, but by the time I had finished it, the author had me convinced. She had argued and detailed such a specific "schema" that the two guys who had written the damned thing with no such *conscious* intent now bought into her thesis. I wrote her a letter thanking her, in all sincerity, for telling me something about my own work I hadn't realized.

By then, you see, the business of people saying what *Bonnie and Clyde* was "really about" had become almost a cottage industry. Articles appeared saying it was "really about" Lee Harvey Oswald. (Why? Guns and Texas?) Others "proved" it resonated because it was "really about" police brutality, a particularly hot topic at that time. Then there were the "really about Vietnam" theorists and "really about the race riots in Watts" crowd. Just last month, a writer from a national magazine interviewed me in connection with the thirtieth anniversary of the film's release. When I mentioned that the Oscar ceremonies that year had been delayed two days out of respect for the assassination of Martin Luther King earlier that week, he instantly seized on that information as "proof" of his theory that what the movie was "really about" was race riots in America. Go know.

I've looked at clouds from both sides now. With the same kind of total confidence, I tried more than once to tell Jean-Luc Godard about some thematic insight I'd found in his work, only to be answered by a silent grin. I soon abandoned the attempts. (Hey, of course, I *am* right, it's just he doesn't know it, y'see?)

Over the years, I've decided to let the theorists theorize because they may be, in some skewed fashion, partly correct. I exempt the guy who came up to me in 1972, with hair even longer than mine was, and said, "Hey, man [the standard greeting of the time, often followed by, 'Got any spare change?'], I saw your movie three times. The first two times I didn't dig it so much, but then the last time I was totally stoned, man, and I suddenly realized it was about this thing with orange!" "Orange? Did you say 'orange'?" He looked at me like I was the village idiot. "Yeah, man, the color orange, the way it keeps coming in different scenes all through the movie. Far out, man! It's a great movie!" I started to explain to this person that whatever he saw in it when stoned, we hadn't written it when we were stoned, nor (as far as I know) was it filmed by anyone in that state, and so he was nuts. Whereupon he got belligerent but in that slow-motion way a joint of Maui-wowee used to cause, so I managed to slip away without "gratuitous violence."

Ah, good old gratuitous violence – the phrase used by every outraged critic in 1967 who didn't understand that the entire point of the violence in our movie was that it was *not* gratuitous, that we were saying that if you chose to make your living as an outlaw you had better know that pain and blood and horror come with the territory. We had gone on in the initial treatment to say that, unlike current Hollywood hokum, we wanted to show that when a bullet penetrates human flesh it hurts like hell and one of the things we intended to do was show that penalty in all its unvarnished truth. And *this* people called "gratuitous"? Or, even dumber, all the complaints that the film "glorified" violence, as if we were saying, "Hey, isn't this neat fun? You get your brains shot out and your mouth bubbles with blood and all you are is a fairly inept bank robber! Wouldn't that be a swell way for all of us to live?"

But I digress. The book you hold in your hand contains a number of learned and no doubt well-thought-out arguments concerning what *Bonnie and Clyde* is really about. I haven't read the contents yet, but I do remember a startling phone call from one of the contributors herein, who had gotten my phone number from Les Friedman, the editor-compiler-guru of this tome. Here's how the conversation began: after introducing herself, she said, "I've just done a 'cold reading' of *Bonnie and Clyde*." "A *what*?" "A cold reading." I had visions of her standing in a meat locker with the screenplay in hand, but it transpired that it was some kind of academic term roughly translated as "seeing it again with fresh eyes." "How so?" I asked innocently. "Well," she answered, "the first time I saw it, when it originally opened, I was a straight teenage girl, but now" – and I could practically finish the sentence in unison with her – "I've seen it again as a lesbian woman in her forties." Pause for reflection on my part. "And?" "And I've come to realize that it is the breakthrough Hollywood film about homosexuality." (If I had tears, prepare to shed them now.) I asked her what in hell she was talking about, and she first cited the one fact that was always a part of the record, written by Benton and me in our introduction to *The*

Bonnie and Clyde Book, published by Simon and Schuster in 1972, and retold by me to the late Vito Russo in his book, *The Celluloid Closet*. For those who don't know it, here's the short version.

In writing the first draft (for reasons to be explained shortly), Bob and I, having spent months researching the true facts and the mythological ones about the Barrow gang and then choosing what we wanted to use or not from both categories, had come across "rumors" that Clyde was a bisexual, at least by the time he had been released from prison. The rumors further intimated, and *intimated* was all they did, that at least *some* of the wheelmen, the guys who drove the getaway car, were forced into a ménage à trois with Bonnie and Clyde, for otherwise Clyde couldn't "function." Since one of our main purposes for choosing to write about this story for our first screenplay was what we thought it was "really about" – the aberrations of style being flaunted at an uptight society – we thought that threesome stuff fit right in. Having already decided to take all the "driver" guys and combine them into one character, our first draft portrayed him as a dumb country stud who was bug-eyed at being dragged into a kind of kinky sex he'd never even imagined.

In fact, neither Benton nor I knew much about this topic or about how the dynamics of such a relationship would truly affect the characters, but anyway it was in the first draft. When, in an oft-told story, the screenplay went through its two years of Truffaut and then Godard development and endless rejections by all the major studios, only to be saved at the bell by Warren Beatty, the very first meeting we had with Warren and Arthur was about that threesome stuff. Warren was adamant about its being removed for two reasons, the first being that it was not such a terrific thing for his image and that audiences wouldn't accept him that way, and the second being that it "just wasn't working." Arthur, though, really nailed it for us: he pointed out (remember, this was 1965, long before the Gay Liberation movement and Gay Pride and all that; it was a time when people commonly called gays "perverts" or worse and conventional

FIGURE 3
Bonnie and Clyde scriptwriters David Newman (*left*) and Robert Benton (1967).

thinking had homosexuality as a sickness) that we risked alienating the audience from what we so badly wanted – that the audience would love and identify with Clyde and Bonnie from the outset, so that by the time the two start doing "violent things," it is too late for the audience to back away from their identification with the desperados. (A classics professor friend of mine calls this "the Medea theory.") Were we to ask the mainstream audience to accept our leading male character as a "pervert," it would allow them to reject all that followed and say, however prejudicially, "Hey, sure he kills people. Whatd'ya expect, the guy's a sicko."

Arthur did agree, however, that we were right in intuiting that Clyde should have some kind of sexual hang-up, and so, in that still-Freudian time, we mutually came up with the notion of impotence, and it was a good solution. It fit right in with all that phallic gun stuff and allowed us to find the moment when Clyde's ego is finally satisfied by the publication of Bonnie's poem, which elevates him to stardom, and thus, for the first time, he can "get it up."

End of subject for me (and for Benton, too). But our dogged contributor said that no, no, there were many more hidden gay subtexts in the film. I was reminded of the guy with the "orange" fixation, and I asked her to name them. She cited as one example the scene in which Clyde passes (in a very crowded room, by the way) C. W. playing checkers with Buck, leans over to kibitz, puts an arm around the kid and then ruffles his hair. "Clearly a homoerotic moment," she said. "Uh-uh," said I who wrote it, "it was meant to be a fraternal gesture." One of the motifs that run through the film is how this artificial family tries to live like a normal bunch, and, whenever they do, they become most vulnerable to attack: "the laws" come riding in, guns blazing, and once again they are forced to abandon domesticity and to take it on the lam. In addition, I suggested, she ought to consult Arthur Penn, who had "blocked" that scene, and that possibly the space allotted in the crossover, as well as the brotherly point we were trying to make, had something to do with the physical proximity of the two guys. Well, she would have none of that, and perhaps her piece in this volume confirms it.

So what is a poor co-scenarist to do? Argue? Instead, I'd like to tell you what Bob and I thought and think *Bonnie and Clyde* is really about.

Bonnie and Clyde is about style and people who have style. It is about people whose style set them apart from their time and place so that they seemed odd and aberrant to the general run of society. Most importantly, they did this by choice. What first attracted us in the mythology was hearing about the photos Bonnie and Clyde took of each other and mailed to the newspapers, the doggerel poetry that Bonnie wrote, the business of Bonnie posing with a cigar, and so on. It was, I still believe, one of the first examples of the now ubiquitous element of American life in which people become famous merely by being famous. It was Andy Warhol's "fifteen minutes of fame" long ahead of its time, for surely their skill as bank robbers was pathetic. But their skill at creating "images" for the public could have gotten them the Coca-Cola account today.

We held that styles and "value systems" that originated in what used to be called "the underworld" inevitably worked their way up to naughty but accepted respectability in what was called "the underground," that is, that whole Andy Warhol/Studio 54 world. It's still true – jargon heard on the basketball courts of Harlem finds its way to the schoolyards of the suburbs within months, at which point the "inner city" invents new lingo to replace it. We felt in writing for *Esquire* the magazine piece entitled "The New Sentimentality" that an entirely new culture was taking hold in America, but nobody had tried to define or codify it. We did. And it led to further exploration of the themes that became the soul of *Bonnie and Clyde*. What we were talking about was what is now known as "the Sixties." But as we were in the midst of living through them at the time, we didn't have a chronological name for what was happening. We felt it, though. If the film is "really about" something, it is about that most of all.

Just as our parents were "offended" by long hair, Woodstock, rock and roll, smoking pot, and dropping out, we reflected this by inventing the tattoo on C. W.'s chest that directly leads to the assassination of Bonnie and Clyde. It isn't, in our movie, because they robbed banks. Poor folk hated the banks, as we went to some pains to illustrate. It isn't because they "broke the law." Ivan, C. W.'s father, doesn't give a hoot in hell about the law. No, what offends him is the way his son shows up with "pictures on his skin," inspired by Bonnie and Clyde. "I'm just glad your ma ain't alive to see that," he barks, constantly obsessed with the tattoo. And because of that (*and only that*), he rats out the luckless couple and sets up the ambush. Because his sense of propriety is offended by their flaunting of a freakish style. Sound like the sixties?

It is also "really about" some factual matters, such as the way the development of the automobile and of roads progressed faster than the changing of laws, enabling police to cross state borders in pursuit. It is about the Depression and about the evocation of "white trash." ("Today on *Sally Jesse* – Backstreet Bandits and the Women Who Love Them!!") It is about what we called "a professional love affair," examples of which did then and still do abound: couples who may not have sexual compatibility but who do know that the partners can help each other to realize their dreams of glory and success. See any current issue of *People* magazine, for nine hundred examples.

Finally, I quote directly from the original treatment we wrote before starting the screenplay, because I can't put it any better today:

> This is a movie about criminals only incidentally. Crime in the 30's was the strange, the exotic, the different. This is a movie about two people, lovers, movers and operators. They're "hung up," like many people are today. They moved in odd, unpredictable ways which can be viewed, with an existential eye, as classic. Their relationship, in fact, is an existential one. Their crimes were against man, and their best moments came because of their commitment to their own humanity.
>
> They are not Crooks. They are people, and this film is, in many ways, about what's going on now.

Five months after that night at Radio City, Arthur Penn and I, along with Estelle Parsons, were invited to the Miami Film Festival to once again view the film and mark its thirtieth anniversary. On a "normal" size screen, the new print looked even better. Following the showing, there was a cocktail party in a very surreal setting: the roof of a bank building, surrounded by

FIGURE 4
The "professional love affair" between Bonnie and Clyde: existentialism with style.

Miami neon. And, standing at the bar, I turned to Arthur and said, "What a long, strange trip it's been." Which is, as you probably know, one of the quintessential lyrics from the Grateful Dead.

In other words, from "the Sixties." One of the things *Bonnie and Clyde* is "really about."

"It's Never the Way I Knew Them"

SEARCHING FOR BONNIE AND CLYDE

"When the legend becomes fact, print the legend."

> *The Man Who Shot Liberty Valance* (1962; *d.* John Ford)

May 23, 1934, Bonnie Parker and Clyde Barrow drove south on Highway 154, heading toward their ramshackle cabin hideout a few miles outside Gibsland, Louisiana. Near the crest of the first steep grade, Ivan "Old Man" Methvin had angled his truck on the edge of the two-lane road where trees and brush crowded up to the shoulder. Spying the father of their friend Henry Methvin, Clyde slowed as he neared Ivan's truck disabled with a flat tire. Two quick shots from Prentis Oakley, a pause, and a barrage of bullets from five more men tore through Bonnie and Clyde and their stolen car. Clyde Barrow probably died with the first shot from the sharpshooter Oakley; perhaps, Bonnie died with the second shot. At any rate, a more than sufficient number of the 167 bullets from the six-man posse found their mark: 52 bullet holes and glass cuts marred Bonnie's body; a couple dozen bullets, one breaking his backbone, hit Clyde, as verified in Dr. J. L. Wade's coroner's report (see Appendix A).

Clyde's head lay at an angle against the door; Bonnie lay slumped against Clyde. With their grisly, violent deaths, Bonnie and Clyde were assured of their place among the pantheon of America's legendary outlaws.

Popular culture perpetuates and embellishes tales of criminals who capture our imagination. And of all the media, cinema most powerfully romanticizes the lives of infamous individuals, reinventing them to the measure of our desire, replacing fact with a compelling fiction that becomes accepted "truth." Accepted "knowledge" holds that Pat Garrett, long-time acquaintance of Billy the Kid, betrayed and murdered Billy in his prime. We "know" that before Jesse James could settle down to a productive life, his trusted friend Bob Ford, a craven coward, shot him in the back. We also believe that, though Butch Cassidy and the Sundance Kid escaped their U.S. pursuers, Butch and Sundance had no chance when a detachment of Mexican troops riddled their bodies with bullets.[1] That we "know" all this with such vivid certainty testifies to the ease with which filmic representation supplies our images, often to the exclusion of more factual interpretations. And when a brutal death befalls a criminal or, for that matter, a prominent figure,[2] we are enthralled by the confrontation with their mortality and reminded of ours. The thirties did not lack harrowing examples.

Throughout the Prohibition/Depression era, flamboyant gangsters wreaked havoc and suffered gruesome deaths, catapulting their scandalous stories into the newspapers and onto cinema screens, intensifying our fascination with them. In December 1931, unidentified assailants murdered Jack "Legs" Diamond with five bullets to his head and body. John Dillinger was machine-gunned to death July 22, 1934, and in April, June, and August of that year, surviving members of Dillinger's gang met similarly bloody ends at the hands of lawmen. The folk hero Charles Arthur "Pretty Boy" Floyd, who probably met Bonnie and Clyde during his travels, was gunned down by FBI agents on October 22, 1943, as he fled on foot. Baby Face Nelson killed two FBI men and was shot to death in November 1934, as in

January 1935 were Ma Barker and her son Fred. This list of re-
nowned desperadoes must include two who died on May 23,
1934, when a six-man posse wrote an exceedingly grotesque
final act for the already sensationalized Bonnie Parker and Clyde
Barrow. With death, tales of these disreputable individuals
slipped irretrievably from accurate portrayal into lurid legends,
the struggle for accuracy subordinated to titillating, vicarious
entertainment.

As happened with other popular outlaws, many familiar and
several unique aspects of Bonnie and Clyde's story enhance the
couple's widespread, enduring appeal. Like the others, Bonnie
and Clyde exemplified the intrinsic drama of violence, fast cars
(the gang member Ralph Fults boasted that Clyde "was one with
the machinery"[3]), and powerful guns (Clyde preferred BARs,
Browning Automatic Rifles). Distinctively, they offered the romantic relationship of an attractive young man and woman on
the run; more than two years of improbable escapes from Texas
prisons and ambushes; the kidnapping and release of law officers
and civilians; two spectacularly wild shootouts, one involving
an armored car (July 18, 1933, Platte City, Missouri); lower-class
origins; and Depression bravado. Their short, elusive, fierce lives
provided all the elements sufficient for mythic fabrication and
moral instruction.

But in 1934, Bonnie and Clyde's notoriety, augmented
through extensive newspaper coverage across the Midwest and
the Southwest and, to a lesser extent, throughout the nation,
scarcely needed reinforcement. First via print journalism and
then on radio, quickly via popular books and in films, soon on
television and in academic scholarship, Bonnie and Clyde's activities have been reported, misrepresented, magnified, carica-
tured, discussed, and dissected. Every one of these inevitably
reveals a bias and an explicit or implicit agenda. Some journalists
get basic facts wrong. Some authors deliberately slant their interpretations to create exciting profiles. Some writers and directors
take poetic license to attract audiences. Atypically, Bonnie and
Clyde themselves submitted poems and photographs to news-

FIGURE 5
Bonnie Parker and Clyde Barrow. Courtesy of Texas/Dallas History and Archives Division, Dallas Public Library.

papers to further their self-aggrandizement. But the absence of first-person interviews and of bold media exposure that might limit, defuse, or even fortify their appeal reinforces the couple's mysteriousness, enhancing their celebrity. For the sixty years after their deaths, their lives have offered malleable material for interpretation and reinterpretation (as Arthur Penn's *Bonnie and Clyde* also proves).

From the beginning, the explanation of Bonnie and Clyde's lives has involved many individuals struggling to perpetuate *their* versions. As Clyde's younger sister Marie astutely observed, "I guess there's something about a girl and a boy . . . but nobody has ever really told the story as I knew them. It's always been some other story they told, lies."[4] Marie Barrow and scores of reliable, meticulous authorities must realize that the "truth" is irrelevant to good storytelling, compelling cinema, and a legend's perpetuation. If details contradict the "story," the tale nevertheless triumphs. In addition, knowing that film and television often surrender complexity to striking visuals, several recent books detail the strengths and weaknesses of filmic versions of history. Even the widely praised, award-winning PBS *Civil War* series provoked unprecedented controversy.[5] As the film theorist Bill Nichols writes concerning documentary film (an observation applicable to all narrative), "The notion of any privileged access to a reality that exists 'out there,' beyond us, is an ideological effect. The sooner we realize all this, the better."[6]

We add to this important awareness the certainty that all historical inquiry also highlights the difficulty of determining exactly what happened, how it happened, and why, even when eyewitnesses still live and the project's aims are noble. At best, an account reflects the benefits from untiring efforts for accuracy, the investigator ever wary that the desire to deliver a compelling account not surrender precision to thrilling characterization or self-interest. Inevitably, the nature of the tale finally told reveals a great deal about the people and the times that produced it.

From late 1991 through May 1994, I conducted research and contributed to the production of the hour-long documentary

Remembering Bonnie and Clyde.[7] The late director-writer-producer Tim Leone and I surveyed hundreds of articles in newspapers and magazines, read the voluminous material that constitutes Dallas sheriff Richard Allen "Smoot" Schmid's scrapbook, studied the FBI report,[8] watched strikingly different depictions in early and recent films, and conducted phone and in-person interviews with the few remaining eyewitnesses and secondhand sources. Our research reinforced our belief in the inclination of many "average folks" to mythologize daring criminal activity.[9]

Of the dozens of individuals to whom I spoke in two and a half years of research and production on *Remembering Bonnie and Clyde* (see Appendix B), everyone responded with interest in the couple. Reenactments of nefarious events in the lives of Bonnie and Clyde, including their robberies, take place with regularity in various locations. "Bonnie and Clyde Days" are celebrated every fall outside Arcadia, Louisiana; newsletters prosper; web pages proliferate; the Arts and Entertainment and Discovery channels have run documentaries on the pair; as recently as fall 1993 the *Texas Highway Patrol Association Magazine* ran an article on the first two Texas highway patrol troopers murdered by Bonnie and Clyde.[10] Even Kato Kaelin, who became famous as O. J. Simpson's houseguest, poses for *Esquire* dressed like Clyde, and proclaims in *GQ* (August 1995) that Penn's *"Bonnie and Clyde* was my passion into teenhood" (p. 177).

Six years after we began our intensive research, I'm less sure than ever who Bonnie and Clyde were but more clear about who many individuals want them to be. Pervasive themes emerge, almost an X-ray of American passion for independence, rebellion, and defiance. To borrow from Joseph Campbell's analysis of myth, "People say that what we're all seeking is a meaning for life. . . . I think that what we're seeking is an experience of being alive, so that our life experiences on the purely physical plane will have resonances within our own innermost being and reality, so that we actually feel the rapture of being alive."[11] Bonnie and Clyde's "career" of crime obliges.

Clyde's sister Marie expressed love and empathy. The gang

member Ralph Fults was impressed by Clyde's mechanical and driving expertise. The opinion of Gibsland residents who observed Bonnie and Clyde alive and then dead range from disgust with their crude, common lives to mild curiosity and amazement at their notoriety. The coroner's report is factual and sufficiently gruesome to shock. Newspaper articles take moral stands as does the reenactment released two months after their murder. From 1934 to 1997, every observation reveals the complex morass of details *and* the struggle to dominate discourse.

Reacting to negative reports about Bonnie and Clyde, loyal family and friends scathingly condemned pejorative elements, as Marie Barrow illustrates best. "Clyde was a tender-hearted boy and he loved his mother more than anything in the world. . . . We were a real close family. . . . They called [Clyde] a cold-blooded killer and he definitely was not a cold-blooded killer. . . . It was the newspapers trying to make a dollar,"[12] she insisted. One is tempted to say that the families of the twelve or thirteen people killed by Clyde would have another characterization of him, another story, which is exactly the point. The following representative examples from newspapers and the unique contributions of those interviewed illustrate the struggle for and difficulty of arriving at a coherent version of Bonnie and Clyde's story.

THE FBI REPORT, 1930s NEWSPAPER COVERAGE, AND FIRSTHAND ACCOUNTS

Of the FBI's 461 pages devoted to Bonnie and Clyde, to their exploits and their legacy from 1933 through 1935, most of the headlines and many of the subheadings are readable. The texts of almost all the articles, however, are illegible, not because of faulty reproduction but because of the deteriorated condition of the original newspaper documents. The file of the FBI (called the Bureau of Investigation in the early 1930s) also contains a legible wanted poster dated May 21, 1934, citing the National Motor Vehicle Theft Act. The poster has several factual errors

FIGURE 6
Clyde with his mother, Cumie Barrow. Courtesy of Texas/Dallas
History and Archives Division, Dallas Public Library.

concerning the two outlaws. For example, Clyde's middle name was Chestnut, not Champion; Bonnie was barely 5 feet, not 5 feet 5 inches; and descriptions of scars and wounds were guesses. The warning about the need for extreme caution came from experience and the death toll left in Bonnie and Clyde's wake.

The report's cover sheet, dated December 14, 1934 (revised October 1983), establishes its own perspective, describing Bonnie and Clyde's last days as "one of the most colorful and spectacular manhunts the Nation had seen up to that time." Asserting that the bureau became "interested in Barrow and his paramour late in December 1932" over interstate transport of a stolen car taken from Texas to Oklahoma, a warrant was issued for them May 20, 1933, barely one year before their ambush. Surprisingly, the newspaper articles collected reflect a less inflammatory tone than the bureau's own description.

Given the number and popularity of gangster films in the 1930s and the pressure to teach a moral lesson (resulting in the 1934 Production Code), it is not startling to see newspapers using outlaw tales to warn their readers of the dire consequences of criminal behavior. The *St. Paul Dispatch*, for example, repeatedly ran stories with the banner "Crime Does Not Pay." Newspapers used Bonnie's and Clyde's deaths to taunt John Dillinger and Pretty Boy Floyd, for example, "Killing of Couple . . . Shouts to Dillinger and Floyd: 'You Can't Get Away with It.' " To reinforce the warning, several newspapers quoted Bonnie's twenty-one-year-old sister, Mrs. Billie Mace, as saying, "I'm not surprised. I've been expecting it to end this way." (Ironically, Billie spoke from jail after her own arraignment on charges stemming from the murder of the two highway patrolmen outside Grapevine [near Dallas], Texas. She was later released.) While the stories posted warnings and drew moral conclusions, the sensational nature of Bonnie and Clyde's exploits sold papers.

Contemporary reports stressed Mrs. Parker's realization that Bonnie "knew she would be killed. She knew they wouldn't last long. But there was nothing else to do but keep driving all the time" (*St. Louis Post Dispatch*, May 24, 1934). Echoing these sentiments, in 1993 Marie Barrow commented, "I didn't feel anger toward the officers because I knew that sooner or later he [Clyde] was going to get killed; he knew it, all of us knew it."[13] Clyde was described as "Just a Drugstore Cowboy Whom Petty Crime Made a Killer" (*St. Louis Star-Times*, May 23, 1934). "First booked by Police at Age of 16 – Arch-Desperado Aided in Killings and Robberies by Cigar-Smoking 'Suicide Sal.' " Bonnie hated the depiction of her as a "cigar-smoking" woman, a degrading (and erroneous) detail headlines exploited.

Newspapers covered the exploits of Bonnie and Clyde comprehensively for the two years that the pair fled the police. But the greatest coverage followed the ambush, which had been witnessed only by the six posse members and, perhaps, Ivan Methvin. The *St. Louis Star-Times*, May 23, 1934, announced, "Officers Ambush Outlaws," followed by the subheading, "Pair Never Got Chance to Fire." The *St. Louis Globe Democrat* led with "Barrow and Woman Companion Slain in Louisiana Ambush"; its subheading was "Fifty Bullets from Old-Time Texas Ranger and Country Sheriffs Riddle Pair as They Speed Along Highway." Typical of the hyperbole dominating such stories, the *New York Times*, May 24, 1934 (the day after the ambush), ran a headline, "Barrow and Woman Are Slain by Police in Louisiana Trap," with the subheading, "Bandit Pair Are Riddled With Bullets as Car Speeds at 85 Miles an Hour." In fact, Clyde must have been driving slowly, based on the trap of Old Man Methvin, the nature of the rural roads, and the condition of the car after their murder. Frank Hamer, in charge of the posse, said that Clyde was not driving over thirty miles an hour (*St. Louis Post Dispatch*, May 24, 1934), and a reporter quotes posse member Manny Gault reporting the speed as forty miles an hour. But this was the period of yellow journalism, which served up the exploits of Prohibition gangsters and desperado escapades, and facts were regularly, unabashedly sacrificed to embellish the story.

Photographs and visual images recorded crowd activity and fed media coverage of the deaths of Bonnie and Clyde. The spotlight also shone on the posse members who, according to

FIGURE 7

The posse. *Back row from left:* Ted Hinton, Prentis Oakley, "Man-nie" (Manny) Gault. *Front row from left:* Bob Alcorn, Henderson Jordan, Frank Hamer. Courtesy of Texas/Dallas History and Archives Division, Dallas Public Library.

several sources, posed for hours for pictures and gave numerous interviews. Their bravery, their laments over the murders, especially over Bonnie's, and their admirable courage reinforced through repetition are for their public image. One article included a now-famous comment from the former Texas Ranger Frank Hamer, who was identified as a "nerveless manhunter": "I hate to bust a cap on a woman . . . however, if it hadn't been her, it would have been us." Other articles also emphasized that the "Ex-Ranger 'Hated to Shoot Woman, Especially When Sitting Down,' But Had No Choice" (*St. Louis Post Dispatch*, May 24, 1934). In this same newspaper edition, the poem attributed to Bonnie, "The Story of Bonnie and Clyde," appeared (see Appendix C), accompanied by two photographs, one a shot of the "bullet-riddled automobile" and next to it a playful snapshot of Bonnie holding a sawed-off shotgun on Clyde.

Articles like these emphasized the "murderous career of Clyde Barrow and his blonde gunwoman," the cunning of the ruse that led to their deaths, and the regret that the "country sheriffs" and the former Texas Ranger had had no choice. "The officers gave the bandits the same medicine they had meted out to their victims in more than a dozen fights and raids against the law in which twelve men were killed." In an article syndicated from Arcadia, Frank Hammer reemphasized, "I hated to shoot a woman – but as I looked down my rifle barrel I remembered that Bonnie Parker had taken part in the murder of nine peace officers." He added, "I raised up and commanded them to halt. At the same instant, Clyde reached for his 12-gauge sawed-off shotgun, leaning on the seat between him and Bonnie, and Bonnie reached for a 16-gauge sawed-off shotgun."[14] Hamer's comments reinforce the importance of the sense of fair play that we apply to our storied peacemakers.

Another posse member's book contradicts Hamer's statement. Ted Hinton confesses that the posse knew the condemnation they would receive if their actual behavior were immediately revealed, and thus they hid the truth. Hinton, respected by everyone involved, from Marie Barrow to Clyde's father to other lawmen, as an upstanding person, describes the trap laid for Bonnie and Clyde. In *Ambush: The Real Story of Bonnie and Clyde*,[15] Hinton confirms what Prentis Oakley told his Gibsland neighbor H. M. Parnell. No warning to "stop or we'll shoot" was ever either contemplated or given. [16] The story was concocted to protect the lawmen from recrimination, for doing what they strongly believed was necessary. It also fits the mythic narrative straight out of Western movies, an association fostered by descriptions of ex-Ranger Hamer and the "posse" meticulously staking out a trap.

Articles and film footage from May 1934 and interviews conducted in 1993 confirm an interest not unlike today's in macabre events, testimony to Bonnie and Clyde's renown. "Curious Climb Trees to See Barrow's Body," the *St. Louis Post-Dispatch* wrote on May 25, 1934. The subhead was "Others begin gathering at dawn for glimpse of slain Bonnie Parker." Literally thousands (some estimate 6,000) gathered in Arcadia outside the Wilder's furniture store where the bodies of Bonnie and Clyde were prepared for the families to take them home, which they did the following day. There, "Barrow Rites Today; Time Is Kept Secret" because "Dallas Undertaking Parlor Is Stormed by Curious Citizens." The Parkers did not attend Clyde's funeral and refused to allow Bonnie to be buried at his side;[17] the Barrows did attend Bonnie's memorial. So did thousands of inquisitive citizens. Bearing witness, sharing in a public mourning, satisfying curiosity, and participating in public ceremony are important in marking the passing of a hero or an antihero.

THE STORY'S SPIN

For individuals with strong emotions and businesses with commercial interests, the struggle for control of *the* interpretation began immediately. Determined to modify the couple's reputations and "correct the record," Bonnie's mother, Emma, vowed, less than a month after Bonnie's death, to write the book that would tell the " 'Truth' of Lives of Clyde Barrow and His Partner in Crime," as reported in Dallas, June 11, 1934. To that end, Emma Krause Parker and Clyde's sister Nell Barrow Cowan wrote "The true story of Bonnie and Clyde, as told by Bonnie's mother and Clyde's sister," published in 1934 as *The Fugitives*.[18] According to the Dallas newspapers, Mrs. Parker objected to the posse's behavior: "What do you think of a bunch of men that would shoot them up like that? Shot them from ambush, that's what they did. Didn't give them a chance. They got a signal when to start shooting and didn't even try to take them alive." This account, so transparently filtered through the subjective predisposition of its teller, testifies to the overriding

FIGURE 8
The "death car" after it was towed to Arcadia. Courtesy of
Texas/Dallas History and Archives Division, Dallas Public Library.

importance of ideas of fair play. But in myth, the codes and rules
of poetic justice must be reaffirmed.

Still cashing in on Bonnie and Clyde's fame, newspapers continued their coverage. For over a year after their deaths, Bonnie
and Clyde remained headline news, primarily through the continuing criminal activities of, and legal action against, their, "associates." Headlines kept tantalizing stories alive. "Barrow Be-
trayer Guilty of Murder," reads the lead (Miami, Oklahoma)
reporting the conviction of Henry Methvin, the friend whose
father had arranged the ambush. At his trial, Methvin blamed
Bonnie and Clyde for the April 6 murder of Constable Cal Cam-
ble, between Miami and Commerce, Oklahoma (Methvin was
found guilty of that slaying). But Henry merely followed W. D.

Jones's lead. W. D., who had been in custody in Dallas beginning November 15, 1933, and was defending himself against an indictment for the murder of Deputy Malcolm Davis of Fort Worth, went on film shortly after the ambush to assert that he had been held hostage by Bonnie and Clyde for months. The film recording of his declarations contributed to the Bonnie and Clyde myth without reference to W. D.'s own honesty or motivation.

Sensationalizing other grisly details, newspapers in April 1935 reported, "Convicts Take Barrow's Idea," with a subheading explaining, "Six at Texas Prison Farm Maimed Themselves" (April 4, 1935), referring to Clyde's having persuaded a fellow inmate to chop off two of Clyde's toes so Clyde could get released from a work detail while he was serving time in the dreaded Eastham prison (just outside Huntsville, Texas). At the same time, an Associated Press headline appeared in newspapers from the *Kansas City Star* to the *New York Sun*. "The late desperado Clyde Barrow was blamed today for introducing the self-mutilation at the Eastham Prison Farm where several convicts have chopped off their feet." So heinous was the prison's reputation that long before Clyde's arrival inmates had been taking drastic action, including self-mutilation, to get transported anywhere away from Eastham.

Frank Hamer continued to add to and enjoy his reputation. The *Dallas Morning News* (March 10, 1935) proclaimed, "Nemesis of Killers Is after Hamilton: Sure-Shot Ex-Ranger Who Slew Barrow and Bonnie on Trail," referring to Hamer's pursuit of Raymond Hamilton, a onetime Barrow gang member. And "Barrow Pal Guns Ways Out of Trap," said the *Dallas Daily News*, February 5, 1935, concerning Hamilton. Giving banner headlines to outlaw escapes, the newspapers exploited associations with Bonnie and Clyde.

The families also received coverage as the *Chicago Daily Times* (February 26, 1935) followed the trial of family and friends who had aided Clyde and Bonnie, reporting, "U.S. Convicts 15 Kin and Aides of Slain Outlaw: Found Guilty at Dallas of Harboring

Barrow and Bonnie Parker." Sentences were light, but the infamous names continued to command attention even in the *New York Times* (February 27, 1935): "20 Are Sentenced As Barrow Aides. Mothers of Bandit Leader and Bonnie Parker Among Those Sent to Prisons. All Relatives or Friends. Terms Ranging From One Hour [for Marie Barrow] to Two Years Imposed by Texas Federal Judge." Wanting to prove that "Crime Doesn't Pay," as previous headlines and the 1934 film *The Retribution of Clyde Barrow and Bonnie Parker* had proclaimed, news stories may, unwittingly this time, have suggested the opposite.[19]

THE STORY AS IT IS TOLD AND RETOLD

Several familiar themes recur in the hundreds of headlines compiled in the FBI file on Bonnie and Clyde, the numerous scrapbooks kept at the time by Sheriff Smoot Schmid, the film and books that appeared within months of the murders, and the accounts of friends and relatives. The dominant motif emphasizes romance, speed, and destruction. A young man and a young woman (Clyde 25, Bonnie 23), having eluded law officers for months, are traveling at an extremely high rate of speed in a stolen automobile when they are ambushed and gruesomely slaughtered. This was the first time a woman was murdered along with her male companion. Newspapers highlighted this extremely unusual aspect of the case, repeating that Bonnie had a machine gun in her lap (all other evidence suggests otherwise; they had little reason to suspect any trouble at 9:15 that morning) and describing Bonnie frequently as a "cigar-smoking sweetheart" and as Clyde's "gun girl." These details reinforce Bonnie's role in the relationship as an equally loathsome figure. (In fact, the only confirmed evidence of Bonnie shooting along with Clyde came from the Joplin shootout.) Most descriptions of Bonnie serve to defeminize her, to emphasize her cruder, more masculine behavior, and to marginalize her conformity to 1930s female norms. In contrast, her pictures and firsthand descriptions of her show her as an attractive, small woman.

Pushing for a new angle, one Dallas newspaper article connects Bonnie to the Western myth, making a comparison between her and Annie Oakley, "Modern Gun-Girls Not Much of a Novelty." *The Retribution of Clyde Barrow and Bonnie Parker* echoes this connection, describing Bonnie in voice-over narration as "the worst woman bandit since the days of Belle Starr, the only woman gunned down by the law in attempted capture." The connection with showbiz personalities suggests the creation of Bonnie and Clyde figures, much like the "carny" characters Annie Oakley, Buffalo Bill, and others.

The second most repeated motif in the articles and headlines, added to the three elements just cited, is that of the traitorous, Judas figure, the close friend of Bonnie and Clyde, Ivan Methvin. For example, on May 24 the *St. Louis Post-Dispatch* ran the headline "Supposed Friend Betrayed Barrow for $2500 Reward," with the subheading, "Desperado and Bonnie Parker Speeding Along, So They Thought, to Party When Killed."

The theme of regret recurs in comments from family members, especially Bonnie's regrets as communicated to and by her mother. In a report filed from Dallas, Mrs. Parker said Bonnie "wrote me time and again and said: 'Mother, I'd give anything in the world if I could come home but I can't. I've gone too far. I'd be glad to live on bread and water the rest of my life if I could come home and be like I always was.' But they were too 'hot' then. She didn't kill anybody or hurt anybody." This and other letters and comments by Bonnie suggest she too was helpless to fight the story already accepted. Before her death, Bonnie was already transformed.

CONCLUSIONS

Frank Hamer gives extensive interviews for reporters. Bob Alcorn writes his own version of events for the newspaper. Mrs. Barrow grieves visibly at the funeral, and Bonnie's mother, Emma Parker, and sister Nellie May publish *The Fugitives*, giving

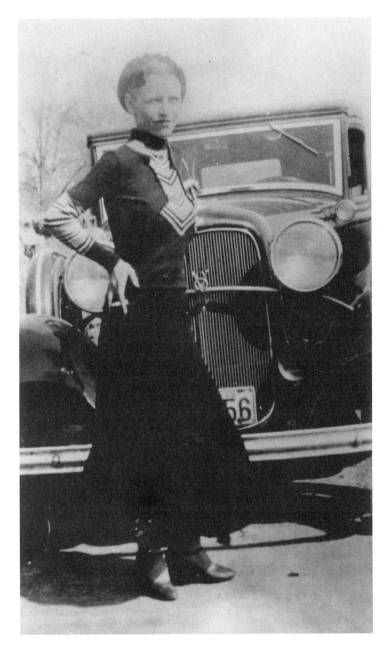

FIGURE 9
Bonnie Parker, five feet tall, posed by Clyde before one of the cars. Courtesy of Texas/Dallas History and Archives Division, Dallas Public Library.

their interpretation of events and of their misunderstood Bonnie.

Hamer added to the fictitious accounts circulating about Bonnie and Clyde with his book, *I'm Frank Hamer*, in which he fabricates motivations and events as easily as he exaggerates his own role. The *St. Louis Globe Democrat*, the *St. Louis Post-Dispatch*, and several other newspapers correctly noted that Frank Hamer was a former Texas Ranger. By several accounts, he quit as a Texas Ranger (others say he was fired) because he would not take orders from the first woman governor of Texas, Maud Ferguson. As reported in contemporary newspapers, Hamer told the *Daily Oklahoman* (May 28, 1934) he quit because "merit no longer counted[;] loyalty to the ruling fashion" held sway. By any standard, he and many others treated prisoners badly. Clyde, a product of the Texas prison system, was proof that the "justice system" intensified the deviant traits of an individual who was already antisocial, just the kind of spectacle the public enjoys.

Before his death from a brain tumor in 1977, Ted Hinton dictated *Ambush*, which appeared in 1979. In his book, Hinton asserts that because the posse broke the law in ambushing Bonnie and Clyde, the six agreed that the last one alive would tell the "truth." He underestimated the appeal of the tale and overestimated the public's regard for accuracy.

Today, because of cinema's power in general and Arthur Penn's persuasive artistry in particular, his film now defines for many Bonnie and Clyde. As film theorists and historians repeatedly assert, and sometimes bemoan, a work's visceral impact often overwhelms intellectual knowledge and critical analysis. So although, as Marie Barrow says, "No one has ever told the true story in my opinion," no one could do so because no legend will sustain it. What is cinematically compelling now dominates historical, biographical, or journalistic discourse.

No one of my research sources explains alone why such unromantic lives hold such universal appeal. In fact, Bonnie and Clyde's circumstances were mundane, if not unattractive, including their final, roughly two-year, spree. Why, then as now, are we so determined to turn common criminals into heroic, liberated Robin Hoods? Perhaps the impulse to mythologize reveals our own repressed frustration at society's restrictions. Perhaps it is the total of all the elements converging in Bonnie and Clyde: their nervy bravado; their elusiveness on the back roads of the Southwest; the tough times of the Depression and their lack of money; a rebellion prompted by the failure of Prohibition and the fame of bootleggers and gangsters; their youth and the romantic appeal of two physically attractive individuals; the involvement of guns; their devotion to their families; and even their independence from an organized, large-scale "mob."

Their reckless actions, their murders of law enforcement officers, the fantasy of their sexual indulgence (one ridiculous rumor had it that Bonnie was pregnant when she was murdered; others said she and Clyde were going to move to Mexico and settle down and raise a family) – all appeal to fantasies at odds with our relatively routine lives. Their larger-than-life escapes from several ambushes and their final gruesome end prove that, indeed, luck runs out, that "Crime Doesn't Pay," and we reconcile ourselves to law and order. Their lives grab attention in part because we know nothing of their introspection or of any interior struggles to compare to ours. And villains continue to compel more interest than angels.

Marie Barrow deserves the last word. Speaking about the Penn movie, she says: "It was a silly movie, it was really silly . . . but no one has ever really told the true story, in my opinion. It's always been some kind of lie. It was the newspapers trying to make a dollar. They're dead now, they should let them rest, but they don't."[20] No, we don't. But their lives have never mattered as much as the legend they initiated and the one perpetuated by others.

DEDICATION

For fifteen years Tim Leone welcomed my filmmaking students at Turquoise Productions, sharing his encyclopedic knowledge gained from over thirty years in the business. Tim generously counseled and sometimes even hired my students. When he suggested we collaborate on a documentary, I leapt at the opportunity. Over the years that it took to research and produce *Remembering Bonnie and Clyde*, Tim guided and completely financed the project – good, as always, to his word. When Tim died, very prematurely, in July 1997, I feared I could never finish this article. For him I did and in loving memory of Tim I dedicate it.

APPENDIX A
ABBREVIATED CORONER'S REPORT

Clyde C. Barrow: [Several tattoos are noted, including an anchor and a shield and USN. Clyde was never in the navy.] Gunshot wound in head entering front of left ear, exit about 2 inches above right ear. One entered at edge hair above left eye. Several shots entering left shoulder joint. Small glass cut at joint, right hand. 7 small bullet wounds, inner of right knee. A number of glass cuts. Gunshot wound entering fleshy portion, left thigh. 8 bullet wounds striking right side back, from base of neck to angular right scapula to backbone. One striking midway back, breaking backbone.

Bonnie Parker: 2 Diamond rings. 1 ["wrist watch" begun here, then partially deleted]. Gold wedding ring, 3rd finger, left hand. Small watch on left arm, 3-acorn brooch on dress in front, 1 Catholic Cross under dress. Red dress & red shoes. Tattoo on right leg, 2 hearts with arrow, 6 inches above right knee. "Roy" on right, "Bonnie" on left side. Gunshot wound edge of hair about 1½ inches above left eye; another entered mouth on left side. Made exit at center of top skull + another about middle and just below left jaw bone. Another entering above clavicle, left side, ranging into neck. Another entering about 2 inches below inner side left shoulder. 2 bullet wounds, one about 2 inches below left shoulder, another midway arm, fracturing the bone. Another wound elbow left arm, breaking into joint. Another shot in left breast going to chest, 4 inches below axilla [armpit]. 1 shot entering left ibid., 4 inches below [armpit], breaking ribs. 6 shots entering three inches, back region of left scapula. 5 bullet wounds about middle of left thigh. Number of cut places on left leg. Scar apparently from burn 6 inches in length about 3½ width on outer center of right thigh, appears effect of burns. Flesh wound inner side of right knee. Bullet wound right leg about midway, ankle and knee. Another bullet wound, anterior ankle, inner aspect foot, about 2 inches above base of great toe. Gunshot wound, bone of first finger, another middle finger, at bone, severing the member. (*Source:* Carroll Y. Rich, *The Death and Autopsy of Bonnie and Clyde* [n.p.: Carroll Y. Rich, 1990]. The spelling in Dr. Wade's report has been corrected by me.)

APPENDIX B
REMEMBERING BONNIE AND CLYDE

The fifty-eight minute documentary referred to in this article, *Remembering Bonnie and Clyde* (1994), can be purchased by writing CTL Productions, 794 Crescent Woods, Valley Park, MO 63088. A two-hour interview with Marie Barrow was conducted by the producer-director Tim Leone in the production of this video. Also in the documentary are excerpts from interviews conducted by Diane Carson with seven residents of the Gibsland/Arcadia area. These individuals are:

1. Mildred Cole Lyons, a student in the grade school at the time. She jumped on the running board of the death car while Bonnie's and Clyde's bodies were still inside as it was towed through Gibsland to Arcadia, the Bienville Parish seat.
2. Buddy Goldston, the passenger in a lumber truck that pulled out of the woods behind Bonnie and Clyde as they drove to their death.
3. James Cole and LaVohn Cole Neal, brother and sister. Their

father owned a store that Barrow frequented. Clyde bought LaVohn and her cousin an Orange Crush several days before May 24.

4. LaVohn Cole Neal, *see* item 3.
5. H. M. Parnell, a friend of Prentis Oakley and Henderson Jordan.
6. Olin Jackson, who was plowing within earshot of the murder.
7. Alice Brock, who saw Bonnie days before her murder in Gibsland where they stopped for breakfast at Mrs. Canfield's Cafe. She saw the death car as it was towed through town.

The six posse members were

1. Frank Hamer, ex-Texas Ranger.
2. Ted Hinton, from Dallas, well acquainted with the Barrows.
3. Bob Alcorn, special Dallas deputy, also knew Bonnie and Clyde.
4. Manny Gault, Dallas deputy.
5. Henderson Jordan, Bienville Parish, Arcadia sheriff.
6. Prentis Oakley, Bienville Parish, sharpshooter and sheriff's deputy.

The Barrow gang included, on different occasions: Henry Methvin, Ralph Fults, W. D. Jones, and Raymond Hamilton. Incidents involving and characteristics of each of these gang members appear in the character C. W. Moss in Penn's film.

EYEWITNESSES

Eyewitnesses, interviewed for *Remembering Bonnie and Clyde*, agree that Henry Methvin, who was wanted on two counts of murder in Texas, betrayed Bonnie and Clyde in order to receive consideration on the murder charges against him and for the $2,500 reward. With the help of Henry's father, Ivan "Old Man" Methvin, the Texas deputies set up a trap near Gibsland. Two school children (LaVohn Cole Neal and Mildred Cole Lyons), on different buses the morning of May 23, sometime between 7:30 A.M. and 8:00 A.M., remember seeing Ivan and his truck with what appeared to be a flat tire, and recall the driver of Mildred's bus offering to send help, being told the tire was fixed, and driving on. Similarly, about 9:15 A.M., two witnesses (Buddy Goldston and Olin Jackson) heard two shots, a pause, and a barrage of gunfire. Posse member Prentis Oakley told his friend H. M. Parnell that he had jumped the signal and fired twice before the barrage began. Oakley also told John Cole's father that he was fairly certain his first shot had killed Clyde. Shortly after the murders of Bonnie and Clyde, while waiting for a wrecker to arrive for their car, posse member Ted Hinton, who knew the Barrow family, shot 16-millimeter footage of the "death car."

OTHER NOTEWORTHY EVENTS

Other well-documented and noteworthy events include the following: Clyde and Bonnie's abduction of H. D. Darby, an undertaker, and Sophie Stone. The Joplin shootout (April 13, 1933) was an extraordinary confrontation, with two policemen killed, as was the Platte City shootout. At Dexter, Iowa, police did shoot Buck Barrow and apprehend Blanche. Buck died six days later, June 10, 1933. Bonnie was injured in a car wreck and fire near Wellington, Texas. She required medical attention and limped from then on. After his incarceration at Eastham Prison Farm, Clyde made it his personal campaign to break his friends out; so brutal were the conditions on the prison farm that he and many others before and after him maimed themselves to get out of work details. He returned January 16, 1934, for a successful breakout raid on Eastham.

APPENDIX C
"THE STORY OF BONNIE AND CLYDE"

You have read the story of Jesse James,
Of how he lived and died.
If you still are in need of something to read,
Here's the story of Bonnie and Clyde:

Now Bonnie and Clyde are the Barrow gang,
I'm sure you all have read
how they rob and steal,
And how those who squeal,
Are usually found dying or dead.
    They claim them as cold-blooded killers,
they say they are heartless and mean,
But I say this with pride
That I once knew Clyde
When he was honest and upright and clean.
    They don't think they are too tough or desperate,
They know the law always wins.
they have been shot at before,
But they do not ignore
That death was the wages of sin.
    From heartbreaks some people have suffered,
From weariness some people have died,
But take it all in all,
Their troubles are small
Till they get like Bonnie and Clyde.
    Some day they will go down together,
And they will bury them side by side.
To a few it means grief,
to the law it's relief,
But it is death to Bonnie and Clyde.

APPENDIX D

    Born March 24, 1909, at Ennis, Texas, thirty-five miles
south of Dallas, Clyde was the fifth of seven children. Not much
more than sharecroppers, even in prosperous times, the Barrows
moved to Dallas in the twenties, lived temporarily in free camp-
grounds by the railroad tracks, and opened a gas and service
station. Clyde's criminal record began in earnest in 1926, when
he was age seventeen. In 1930 he went to prison for burglary
and involvement in a car theft ring.
    Bonnie Parker was born at Rowena, Texas, on October 1, 1910,
to a poor family. At sixteen, she married Roy Thornton, whom

she never divorced and who, at the time of Bonnie's death, was in prison for robbery. When Bonnie met Clyde in 1930, Thornton was serving time for murder.

Shortly after Bonnie met Clyde (a jury had already convicted him of seven counts of burglary and auto theft), Clyde went first to Denton, then to Fort Worth, and finally to the jail at Waco, from which he escaped thanks to Bonnie and her cousin's smuggling in a gun to him. Then followed: escape, recapture, Eastham prison, toes chopped off, parole (February 1932), a raid on the Eastham prison, more robberies – banks, stores, service stations – and more car thefts, shootouts, a car wreck and resulting fire that badly burned Bonnie (Wellington, Texas, June 1933), a Sowers (Texas) ambush and a bullet-riddled car featured in newspapers, another raid on Eastham prison, another bank robbery, more killing, particularly of police officers, and the final ambush.

Within two months of the pair's deaths, Jamieson Film Company of Dallas, Texas, using Ted Hinton's death-car footage, produced a fifteen-minute film called *The Retribution of Clyde Barrow and Bonnie Parker*, with "Authentic scenes and episodes in the bandit lives of Clyde Barrow and Bonnie Parker." In what we would today called a docudrama, Jamieson staged scenes with actors in the roles of Bonnie and Clyde. The film chronicles Clyde's parole on February 2, 1932, after serving time for burglary and auto theft, and proceeds through the murder of J. N. Bucher, a grocery store owner, and the killing of two Grapevine motorcycle policemen (presented as cold-blooded and vicious by Bonnie, contrary to other evidence). The reenactment shows two of the posse members, Bob Alcorn and Ted Hinton, at the scene of the ambush. *Retribution*'s reenacted footage stages the shooting by the posse members and then edits in Ted Hinton's 16-millimeter film footage of the death car with Bonnie's and Clyde's bodies and the footage of the horde of guns and ammunition. It proceeds to Dallas sheriff Smoot Schmid's proud introduction of Hinton and Alcorn (both from Dallas), and it ends with the funerals and the mobs that attended them. Voice-over narration presents moral and sexist commentary: "Vanity, thy name is woman." Bonnie and Clyde were, according to the narrator, drinking, making love, and practicing target shooting at birds before the Grapevine shooting.

NOTES

1. Like Bonnie and Clyde, all of these outlaws have also been the subject of numerous Hollywood films, including director Arthur Penn's *The Left-Handed Gun* (1958). Based on Gore Vidal's play, Penn's film is as innovative and unusual a depiction of Billy the Kid as the director's presentation of Bonnie and Clyde.
2. The death of Diana Spencer, Princess of Wales, offers the most noteworthy international example. Unlike the examples cited here, Diana was lavishly praised for her involvement in humane causes. But her untimely death and the world reaction to it surpassed all expectations.
3. See John Neal Phillips's *Running with Bonnie and Clyde: The Ten Fast Years of Ralph Fults* (Norman, OK, 1996), for an informative account of Ralph Fults, one of the gang members.
4. Interview conducted by Tim Leone of Turquoise Productions, September 24 and 25, 1993, in Dallas, Texas.
5. See, for example, George MacDonald Fraser, The *Hollywood History of the World: From "One Million Years B.C." to "Apocalypse Now"* (New York: William Morrow, 1988); Peter C. Rolling, ed., *Hollywood as Historian: American Film in a Cultural Context* (Lexington: University Press of Kentucky, 1983); Robert Brent Toplin, *History by Hollywood: The Use and Abuse of the American Past* (Urbana: University of Illinois Press, 1996); and Toplin, ed., *Ken Burns's "The Civil War": Historians Respond* (New York: Oxford University Press, 1996).
6. Bill Nichols, *Representing Reality: Issues and Concepts in Documentary* (Bloomington: Indiana University Press, 1991), 107.
7. *Remembering Bonnie and Clyde* was written, produced, and directed by Charles "Tim" Leone, Turquoise Productions, St. Louis, MO, copyright 1994.
8. Sheriff Smoot Schmid's scrapbook is available on microfilm in the Dallas Public Library, Archives section. The FBI report is available through the Freedom of Information Act, Privacy Acts Section, U.S. Department of Justice, Federal Bureau of Investigation, Washington, DC 20535.
9. I use "mythologize" in the popular sense of the term, not in the more accurate and formal sense of myth. Still, I believe the drive to

mythologize, to make people and their experiences larger-than-life, derives, ironically, from some of the same impulses. And killing – the way Bonnie and Clyde were killed – reminds us of ritual slaughter as well.

10. Linda Brown, "Murphy and Wheeler," *Texas Highway Patrol Association Magazine* 2, no. 3 (Fall 1993): 34–5, 37, 39.

11. Joseph Campbell, *The Power of Myth*, with Bill Moyers (New York: Doubleday, 1988), 5, 73.

12. Interview by Tim Leone, September 24, 1993.

13. Ibid.

14. Frank Hamer gives a more complete account of his life, as well as his version of the ambush, in *I'm Frank Hamer: The Life of a Texas Peace Officer*, by H. Gordon Frost and John H. Jenkins (Austin: Pemberton Press, 1968). By the descriptions of many, Hamer was a feared, not a revered, presence. According to several accounts, he quit the Rangers rather than take orders from Maud Ferguson, the first woman to be elected Governor of Texas (cited, e.g., in the *Daily Oklahoman*, May 28, 1934). Regarding Hamer, Marie Barrow commented, "I didn't like Frank Hamer. I didn't know him but I didn't like the things I heard about him" (September 25, 1993, interview with Tim Leone).

15. Ted Hinton as told to Larry Grove (Austin: Shoal Creek Publishers, 1979). Marie Barrow commented, "Ted Hinton seemed like a pretty good guy. He tried to help a lot after this happened. I know he tried to find L. C. [the youngest Barrow brother] jobs" (September 25, 1993, interview with Tim Leone). Others noted that Hinton visited the Barrow service station several times after the ambush, offering his condolences to the family.

16. Personal interview, October 8, 1993, Gibsland, Louisiana.

17. Bonnie and Clyde are buried in the Dallas area. Bonnie's grave is located at Crown Hill Park. Across town, Clyde's grave is in Western Heights Cemetery.

18. With an introduction by Nelson Algren. Comp., arr., and ed. Jan I. Fortune (New York: Signet, 1968).

19. Clyde's mother, Cumie T. Barrow, and Bonnie's mother, Emma Parker, each received thirty days. Marie was sentenced to one hour. Hilton Bybee, a gang member and friend, received ninety days. Raymond Hamilton's mother (Raymond was a gang member) received thirty days.

20. Interview by Tim Leone, September 24 and 25, 1993.

From "Fucking Cops!" to "Fucking Media!"

BONNIE AND CLYDE FOR A SIXTIES AMERICA

"MAINSTREAMING DEVIANCY"

In the waning days of Senator Bob Dole's 1996 presidential campaign, the Republican candidate accused the media of defacing "family values." The concept was not exactly new to political discourse. In 1992, less than a week after the Los Angeles violence promoted by the acquittal of police officers videotaped beating Rodney King, Vice President Dan Quayle fretted over Murphy Brown, a fictional character on prime-time television who was having a fictional baby out of wedlock. Never mentioning Candace Bergen, the star of the show, Quayle referred instead to her fictional persona as he spoke before the San Francisco Commonwealth Club. The riots, Quayle bemoaned, resulted from a crisis in family values brought about by the media. Now, three years later and the Los Angeles rebellion a distant memory, Senator Dole took up the standard of family values with renewed vigor. The dangers of sex and violence in the media, particularly for children, loomed larger than ever. "One of the greatest threats to American family values," Dole argued, "is the way our popular culture ridicules them. Our music, movies, television and advertising regularly push the limits of decency, bombarding our children with destructive messages of casual violence and even more casual sex."[1]

Considering the impact *Bonnie and Clyde* (1967) had upon its audience in the late sixties, Dole's stump epistle for the relatively compliant nineties appears a bit overwrought. The Republican candidate accused rap groups like 2 Live Crew and films like Oliver Stone's *Natural Born Killers* (1994) of what he called "the mainstreaming of deviancy."[2] Although not every rap song or movie neatly conforms to the domestic correctness of the conservative agenda, there was certainly more of the mainstream in the alleged deviancy cited by Dole than there was deviancy in the mainstream. The lyrics of 2 Live Crew often hail the group's male listeners with hyper-heterosexual fantasies of objectified women. And had Dole actually watched Stone's movie – a nineties update of the Bonnie and Clyde myth – he might have readily concurred with its rendering of the media as greedy, unethical purveyors of sensationalism.

One should still find cause for concern, both with Dole's speech and with a broader, nonpartisan tendency to promote socalled family values within the media. This concern, arguably, should rest less with any so-called deviancy and more with the *lack* of deviancy in – or even of opposition to – what mainstream contemporary discourse labels as "deviant." *Natural Born Killers* uses some oppositional strategies, but it is no *Bonnie and Clyde* for its time. Given their respective contexts, the two films emerge as very different, in spite of their shared narrative lineage. Oliver Stone's film received a somewhat cool critical and popular reception – although it certainly has its adherents.[3] Arthur Penn's film, on the other hand, stood established film criticism on its head and passionately divided its audience. Todd Gitlin recalls how, at the end of *Bonnie and Clyde*'s Hollywood premiere, an audience member arose from his seat and yelled "Fucking cops!"[4] *This* should have been the film that Dole lambasted, but the Republican candidate had come to power twenty years too late. To shore up his political support, he simply joined a chorus of voices across a diverse political spectrum, all in es-

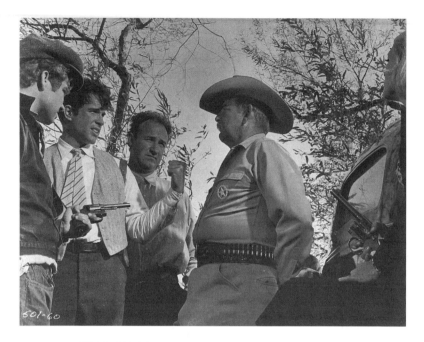

FIGURE 10
"Fucking cops!"

sence yelling "Fucking media!" Dole's unique contribution was
to dub one of the voices in this chorale – the media breast-
beating *Natural Born Killers* – as deviant.

While struggle and resistance have not disappeared from
mainstream popular culture, their place and purpose have
changed since the sixties. Few movies since *Bonnie and Clyde*
have had such a profound impact on the culture or have generated as intense and passionate a debate. With its violent references to sixties culture, its relative sexual frankness for the time,
and its calculated links between repressive forces of the Depression and repressive forces of the sixties, *Bonnie and Clyde* evidenced a "mainstreaming of deviancy" better than Bob Dole
could ever have imagined. The violence in *Natural Born Killers*,
far more graphic than that in Penn's film, also repelled many
viewers. By 1996, however, explicit and graphic depictions of

FIGURE 11

Tommy Lee Jones's prison warden in *Natural Born Killers* (1994) updates Sheriff Hamer.

violence were hardly unique to Stone's film. This violence served a very different purpose from that in *Bonnie and Clyde*. The brutality and anti-Arab racism of another summer blockbuster – the Arnold Schwarzenegger vehicle *True Lies* (1996) – somehow escaped Bob Dole's notice. And Dole praised *Independence Day* (1996) as a promoter of family values, even though (or perhaps because) the violence in that movie claims a flamboyantly gay character, a maternally deficient First Lady, and a mentally unbalanced Vietnam veteran who may or may not have been the victim of male rape.[5] In the nineties, the narrow interests of family values could still promote violence, especially when directed against the "deviant."

If the style of both *Natural Born Killers* and *Bonnie and Clyde* engendered controversy in their respective eras, only *Bonnie and Clyde* could generate controversy by what it said as well as by how it said it. In contemporary reviews, critics contended that both films used excessive violence. Controversy over the graphic nature of these films turned them into what John Fiske has called "media events." As Fiske notes, media events serve as crisis points within culture – connecting, conducting, charging, and redirecting various statements and ideas that constitute discourse.[6] Thus, a discourse on violence and the media runs through *Natural Born Killers* and *Bonnie and Clyde*, charging them with ideological significance. This body of statements and deeply held beliefs connected the two films to ongoing debates over the nature and purpose of violence in the media and made them important.

"THE NEW SENTIMENTALITY" FOR A SIXTIES AMERICA

Bonnie and Clyde appeared in a year, 1967, marked by unprecedented civil ferment, involving both race relations and opposition to the Vietnam War. In 127 U.S. cities during that year, seventy-seven protestors died and four thousand were wounded in clashes between police and citizens. By July, the crisis had peaked in Newark and Detroit. After police arrested and beat a black man following a traffic violation on July 12, 1967, widespread protests shook Newark. Police and National Guardsmen began shooting at anyone who looked black. After five days, all except two of the twenty-six persons killed were black. Thousands were either injured or arrested. Six days later, a police raid on a predominately black club in Detroit resulted in a week of rioting so severe that the city had to summon federal troops. This time, all but seven of the forty-three dead were black. Thousands were either arrested, injured, or left homeless.[7]

The year 1967 also marked a turning point in civic support for the Vietnam War. By February, civil rights leader Dr. Martin Luther King, Jr. had publicly denounced the war. A month later, he referred to the United States as "the greatest purveyor of violence in the world," encouraged draft evasion, and called for stronger ties between the civil rights movement and antiwar protests.[8] Many individuals participated in a series of massive antiwar protests throughout the year. As hundreds of thousands took to the streets across the country – cities such as Washington, DC, New York, Chicago, Philadelphia, Los Angeles, and San Francisco – police responded with mass arrests. Well-known celebrities like the folk singer Joan Baez, poet Allen Ginsberg, and pediatrician Benjamin Spock were also arrested during these protests. On October 21 alone, police arrested 647 protestors outside the Pentagon. By November, Lewis B. Hershey, the director of the Selective Service, announced a new retaliatory measure: any male college student arrested in an antiwar demonstration would automatically lose his draft deferment.[9] Meanwhile, a more insidious response to widespread public dissent took shape. The Central Intelligence Agency launched Operation Chaos, in which the agency began to spy upon everyday U.S. citizens. Its efforts culminated in thirteen thousand files containing three hundred thousand names. Anyone remotely associated with protesting the Vietnam War might have his or her letter or telegram opened by the federal government.[10]

Despite, or arguably as a result of, such heavy-handed actions, a wave of counterculture was about to crest in the mass media ocean. One of the first blockbuster rock concerts was held, the 1967 Monterey Pop Festival, featuring the Grateful Dead and Janis Joplin. By November, the debut issue of the San Francisco–based magazine *Rolling Stone* had given a slick new face to the cultural margins. Even broadcasting afforded new possibilities to voices outside the mainstream. Prompted by complaints about the limits of commercial media, President Lyndon B. Johnson signed the Public Broadcasting Act in November. By creating the Corporation for Public Broadcasting, the act offered an alternative to the sponsor-supported dogma of supply-side mass media.

However, it was the rise of American commercial television in the sixties that ultimately marked significant shifts in public opinion toward what had once been the counterculture. Footage of carnage in Vietnam began to appear on the nightly news, eroding public support for what had once been a popular war. The three major networks also dabbled with programming irreverant shows like *Laugh-In* and *The Smothers Brothers Comedy Hour*, hoping to attract younger audiences. Coverage of the 1968 Democratic Convention in Chicago revealed Mayor Richard Daley's police force beating demonstrators outside the convention hall; police inside also roughed up CBS reporter Dan Rather while he was on the air, further undermining public confidence in government authority.

The motion picture industry was undergoing its own profound transformation, coinciding with the broader countercultural shifts taking place in society. In his *Radical Visions*, Glenn Man outlines three important changes: the breakup of the studio system, the scrapping of the industry's self-regulating Production Code, and the growing presence and influence of postwar European art cinema in this country.[11] Throughout the 1920s, 1930s, and 1940s, five major studios – Paramount, Metro-Goldwyn-Mayer, Warner Brothers, Twentieth Century–Fox, and RKO – built a powerful oligopoly which controlled virtually every aspect of motion picture production. Motion pictures had evolved into a vertically integrated industry in which a handful of powerful corporate players controlled the production, distribution, and exhibition of films.

Since the turn of the century, religious denominations had railed against the perceived moral effects and influence of this oligopoly. The film industry, responding to the threat posed by its critics, created a self-regulatory and censorship arm, the Production Code Administration (PCA). Every film that the studios produced needed approval from this agency. The Production Code reflected the ideological bent of both Depression-era America and the Catholic hierarchy. For example, the code prohibited films "presented in such a way as to throw sympathy with the crime as against law and justice." The code also stipulated that "brutal killings are not to be presented in detail." Other strictures included a wide assortment of representations depicting sex, vulgarity, obscenity, and profanity. "The sanctity of the institution of marriage and the home," for example, was to "be upheld." Any sexually "suggestive postures or gestures" were "not to be shown." Totally "forbidden" was "sex perversion or any inference to it." The *New York Times's* critic, Bosley Crowther, repeatedly railed against the code, as well as against censorship at state and local levels.[12] Yet Crowther just as vehemently opposed *Bonnie and Clyde*, the film that helped bring about the demise of the Production Code by breaking these and other rules that had governed American filmmaking for more than thirty years.[13]

By exercising self-regulation, the studios were able to stave off outside policing and interference – for a time. In 1948, however, the U.S. Supreme Court handed down its Paramount decision, which cleared the way for the Justice Department to pursue vigorous antitrust litigation against the major studios. Rather than continue an already protracted legal struggle with the Justice Department, the studios signed a series of consent decrees. Ultimately, these decrees forced the major studios to relinquish the exhibition arm of their industry.

Once studios no longer owned vast theater chains, the industry practice of self-regulation began to erode. Post–World War II audiences had relatively unprecedented access to an influx of European art films. No code had governed the making of these movies, now showing in newly independent theaters. One Italian film, *The Miracle* (1950), told the story of a pregnant peasant woman who believes her illegitimate child is the new Christ. Crowther championed this film, and when the New York State Board of Censors refused to issue it an exhibition permit, the *New York Times* critic figured prominently in a Supreme Court case challenging the board's decision.[14] The Court's landmark 1952 decision gave motion pictures First Amendment protection, something film had not had since the Court's 1915 decision upholding state censorship boards. In so doing, it cleared the way for foreign and independent films to appear in the theaters that had once been controlled by the major studios and their self-regulatory agencies.

Meanwhile, postwar Hollywood began to serve a different function. Each major studio experimented with a variety of widescreen and 3-D processes to differentiate its product from that of television. For example, just three years prior to releasing *Bonnie and Clyde*, Warner Brothers released *My Fair Lady* (1964), which became one of the last of the big-budget musical extravaganzas. Such major studio releases, however, now appeared with growing infrequency. Throughout the 1950s and 1960s, movie stars and directors formed their own independent production companies. The studios began to lease their soundstages to these companies and to distribute their films. Postwar Hollywood cinema like Alfred Hitchcock's *Psycho* (1960), Mike Nichols's *Who's Afraid of Virginia Woolf?* (1966), and Stanley Kubrick's *Lolita* (1962) and *Dr. Strangelove* (1964) increasingly dealt with mature themes and appealed to specialized audiences, even if these particular films could still attract a mass audience. These changes often proved to be a double-edged sword. On the one hand, the studios lost control of their lucrative exhibition arms. Also, television displaced the hold movies and radio had upon the mass audience. Yet leasing studio space, providing distribution resources, and locating increasingly specialized audiences could also be highly lucrative for the studios. To be sure, studios already had adjusted to these changes by the time Warner Brothers released *Bonnie and Clyde* in 1967. But just as definitely, *Bonnie and Clyde* embodied what these changes had begun to bear.

Television proved to be a unique financial boon for the film industry. Anthology dramas, which were performed and broadcast live, inspired television critics to dub the early 1950s "the Golden Age" of American television. Many of the original directors of early television – Robert Altman, John Frankenheimer, Sidney Lumet, and, of course, Arthur Penn – eventually made their way to Hollywood. By the mid-1950s, however, television had shifted away from live programming – which could generate revenue only once – to filmed programming, which could generate revenue over and over again. Thus, film studios could earn profits by leasing soundstage space to television production companies.

Influences upon Arthur Penn's career paralleled many of those shaping the New Hollywood. After returning from overseas service during World War II, Penn attended Black Mountain College, a progressive school for the arts outside Asheville, North Carolina, in 1947. The faculty included some of the most experimental and controversial artists of the day, among them the composer John Cage, dancer Merce Cunningham, artists Willem and Elaine de Kooning, and philosopher Buckminster Fuller. The school also served as a haven for alumni of the German Bauhaus School who had become refugees from Nazism during World War II.[15] Penn, who was initially a student at this remarkable school, taught an informal acting class by the end of his first year. As an instructor, he pioneered the use of a number of cutting-edge techniques for the time, including improvisation and the Stanislavsky method.[16] The latter technique encouraged intimate collaboration between director and actor to help the performer draw upon his or her personal experience to create a character.

Penn began his career in live television, working on such esteemed anthology drama series as *Philco Playhouse* and *Playhouse 90*. Often, these remarkable programs featured an original teleplay each week. Relatively unknown creative personnel like Penn could hone their craft on these live broadcasts as well as garner much critical attention. In 1956, the first season of *Playhouse 90*, Arthur Penn directed *The Miracle Worker*, an original teleplay by William Gibson. The broadcast received so much acclaim that its story was later adapted for Broadway, with Penn as the director. In 1962 Penn directed a film version of the play.

Presumably because of his work in live television during the 1950s, Penn was hired as a media advisor to John F. Kennedy and even directed the third in a series of presidential debates between Kennedy and Richard M. Nixon.[17] Penn thus contributed to the "look" of Kennedy during these 1960 debates. The debates marked a watershed moment in the history of political communication. As the historian Erik Barnouw notes, Kennedy's performance ushered in a new breed of media-savvy campaigners:

> What television audiences noted chiefly was the air of confidence, the nimbleness of mind that exuded from the young Kennedy. It emerged not only from crisp statements emphasized by sparse gestures, but also from glimpses of Kennedy not talking. . . . A glimpse of the listening Kennedy [in reaction shots] showed him attentive, alert, with a suggestion of a smile on his lips.[18]

In their influential 1964 *Esquire* article, two aspiring screenwriters, David Newman and Robert Benton, cite John F. Kennedy as harbinger of what the authors called "the New Sentimentality." The "wise, the intellectual and the taste-making people" loved Kennedy, according to Newman and Benton, "because he was tough, because he was all pro, because he was a man who knew what he wanted and grabbed it." With Kennedy, the authors claim, "the New Sentimentality came out in the open." Newman and Benton also referred to the work of the French and Italian New Wave, including the films of Jean-Luc Godard, François Truffaut, and Michelangelo Antonioni. In Godard's *Breathless* (1959), Jean-Paul Belmondo and Jean Seberg were one of the "Key Couples of the New Sentimentality."[19] The New Sentimentality, according to Newman and Benton, is marked by self-indulgence, vicarious thrills, and personal gain.[20]

At the same time, another influential critical movement was also taking root in the United States. Emerging from postwar France, "auteurism" argued that films were the result of a director's personal expression and view. Particularly in the pages of the journal *Cahiers du Cinéma*, soon-to-be erstwhile critics like Truffaut and Godard outlined their *politique des auteurs*. Taking up the banner in the United States, the *Village Voice*'s critic Andrew Sarris became auteurism's most vociferous proponent.

In its argument that a bad film by a good director would always be more valuable and interesting than a good film by a bad director, auteurism conflicted with more traditional sensibilities. Crowther championed great films; auteurism championed great directors. Against this backdrop of violent political upheavals, institutional shifts, and conflicting tastes, *Bonnie and Clyde* marked a moment of crisis in American culture. The film occasioned a remarkable contest of power, with a variety of voices struggling to be heard, to achieve dominance, and to explain the relevance (or lack thereof) of Bonnie, Clyde, and *Bonnie and Clyde*.

"IT'S REBELLION, NOT RIOT"

While the political, social, and aesthetic context of the sixties provided a backdrop against which to "read" the film, *Bonnie and Clyde* was more than just the right film at the right time. Unlike other contemporary Hollywood releases, *Bonnie and Clyde*'s narrative and stylistic elements allowed for a relatively open set of reading positions that resonated with the social and political shifts of the time. That *Bonnie and Clyde* could be about something other than the historical Bonnie and Clyde, and that audiences could understand this distinction, marks the film as one of the most important of the decade. If nothing else, the film and the controversy that followed its release altered American film criticism for years to come.

Bonnie and Clyde actively encouraged its viewers to interpret the film as more than just a gangster story. One could "read" the film as a commentary upon the turbulent sixties. One could read it as the personal vision of an iconoclastic director. Or, one could read *Bonnie and Clyde* as a shift away from the traditional classical narrative of a Hollywood film and toward the European art film. In addition, these various readings not only could coexist but even could complement one another. All of these readings resulted from the film's unique appeal to the knowing spectator.

In reading *Bonnie and Clyde*, the knowing spectator occupies a relatively privileged position. The knowing spectator connects with the film's irreverent style, its tragicomic tone, its graphic depictions of sex and violence, and its deliberate ambiguities – in short, with its New Sentimentality. Interpreting these narrative and visual strategies, this spectator understands *Bonnie and Clyde*'s analogues: the Depression stands for the sixties, gangsters for the counterculture, the police and banks for the Establishment. In blurring traditional distinctions between high and low culture, the film also relies upon a certain degree of pop-cultural literacy among its viewers. The film's irony, its blatant Freudianism, its references to Keystone Cops slapstick, and its debt to the European art cinema all appeal to the knowledgeable viewer. In short, the knowing spectator apprehends *Bonnie and Clyde* as more than just a literal narrative.

When *Bonnie and Clyde* premiered in August at the 1967 Montreal International Film Festival, however, many reviewers did not know what to make of the film's appeal to the knowing spectator. Writing for the *Saturday Review*, Hollis Alpert notes that while *Bonnie and Clyde* "is exceedingly well made," it does not "make clear [its] attitudes toward the two criminals," something Alpert finds "bothersome."[21] *Variety* complains that the film is "inconsistent," "confusing," and "incongruously couples comedy with crime."[22] In his first of three reviews attacking the film, Bosley Crowther complains that it "is assembled in a helter-skelter fashion and played at an erratic, breakneck speed."[23] While the social commentary of the film is not completely lost upon Crowther, he focuses on its aesthetic elements. According to Crowther, *Bonnie and Clyde* is a "slap-happy color film charade" that misses "the very misery and drabness" marking the Depression of the 1930s.[24] Even more disturbing to Crowther was the movie's reception at the film festival, where audiences "wildly received" the film with "gales of laughter and applause." For Crowther, *Bonnie and Clyde* incited a mob mentality that showed "just how delirious these festival audiences can be."[25] Crowther does recognize *Bonnie and Clyde*'s political and social context as the sixties, but views this "callous and callow" film as "but another indulgence of a restless and reckless taste, and an embarrassing addition to an excess of violence." Because of the turmoil of the late sixties, Crowther questions whether "a film should represent . . . [our] country in these critical times."[26]

A week after its premiere in Montreal, *Bonnie and Clyde* opened in New York, to mixed reviews. Kathleen Carroll of the *Daily News* praises the film as "bold and brassy, brutal and brilliant," yet admits that it would "jolt and disturb" anyone who believes it "romanticizes crime."[27] Archer Winsten of the *New York Post* is more circumspect in his praise. *Bonnie and Clyde*, he observes, "is a movie rich in controversy"; it is both praiseworthy and flawed.[28] Reviews in *Newsweek* and *Time* pan the film, calling it a "squalid shoot-'em for the moron trade" and "a strange and purposeless mingling of fact and claptrap," respectively.[29] Meanwhile, Crowther launched his second missive, calling the film "a cheap piece of bald-faced slapstick comedy that treats the hideous depredations of that sleazy, moronic pair as though they were as full of fun and frolic as the jazz-age cut-ups in 'Thoroughly Modern Millie.' "[30]

Shortly after these initial reviews, the film's distributor, Warner Brothers–Seven Arts, pulled *Bonnie and Clyde* from circulation. In the meantime, however, a groundswell of support for the film emerged. Penelope Gilliatt, writing for *The New Yorker*, suggests that the film "could look like a celebration of gangsters only to a man with a head full of wood shavings."[31] Andrew Sarris of the *Village Voice* responded to Bosley Crowther's reviews more directly. "To use the pages of the *New York Times* for a personal vendetta against a director and actor one doesn't like is questionable enough," Sarris writes. "To incite the lurking forces of censorship and repression with inflammatory diatribes against violence on the screen is downright mischievous." Sarris even places Crowther within the camp of "bigots," those racists who use "the fake rhetoric of law and order." In his criticism of *Bonnie and Clyde*, Sarris argues, Crowther employs a similar discourse and thus legitimates attempts "to lash back at the Negro."[32] Meanwhile, readers of the *New York Times* began to protest Crowther's missives. Harold Imber enters "a strong demurrer" to the *Times* critic, comparing *Bonnie and Clyde* to *The Grapes of Wrath*. Kenneth Feldman turns Crowther's *Thoroughly Modern Millie* comparison against the critic, suggesting that he "runs away" when confronted with "the dark side – the real side" of this era. Charles E. Evans argues that rather than the film's encouraging or glamorizing a life of crime, "the moral of inevitable destruction for anyone launching a career of illegality and violence was made abundantly clear."[33]

In her letter to the *New York Times*'s "Movie Mailbag," Teresa Hayden locates the relevance of *Bonnie and Clyde* in media coverage of the race riots that summer: "During the sad, tragic, ugly riots recently in Newark, Detroit, etc., nice commentators and reporters were shocked at what they described as the 'carnival' atmosphere." Hayden stresses how removed the media were from these events. "It seemed so clear what they were describing and why: 'Have-nots' in 1967 or the 1930's who go 'hog-wild,' incapable of imagining our fine bourgeois world as something they can enter legitimately."[34]

Meanwhile, director Arthur Penn began to defend the film in the press. In an interview with *Variety*, Penn claims that if he were "a French director," his critics "might not have liked the picture but they'd have understood what I was trying to do." Penn also began to address the film's violence, aligning it with the political struggle of blacks in America. In an interview for *Cahiers du Cinéma*, Penn recalls how "five negroes" who attended a screening of the film:

> completely identified with *Bonnie and Clyde*. They were delighted. They said: "This is the way; that's the way to go, baby. Those cats were all right." They really understood, because in a certain sense the American negro has the same kind of attitude of "I have nothing more to lose," that was true during the Depression for Bonnie and Clyde. It is true now of the American negro. He is really at the point of revolution – it's rebellion, not riot.[35]

Once *Time* and *Newsweek* reversed their critical assessments of the film, its producer and star, Warren Beatty, convinced Warner Brothers–Seven Arts to re-release the film.[36] A new advertising campaign for the film made much of *Newsweek*'s reversal. And according to *Variety*, studio executives strongly hinted that Bosley Crowther's reviews, reader backlash, and impassioned defenses of the film in other publications all "helped the picture rather than hurt it." As *Variety* notes, even the *Catholic Film Newsletter* of the National Catholic Office for Motion Pictures praised *Bonnie and Clyde*, recommending the film, along with a reissue of *Gone with the Wind*, as the "Best of the Month."[37] Meanwhile, the film was doing phenomenally well in London. According to the London *Observer*, the film "has broken every record" at the movie theater there. In three weeks, the paper estimated that one hundred forty thousand people saw the film.[38]

In the United States, Pauline Kael's career-making defense of the film also marked a turning point for *Bonnie and Clyde*. "How do you make a good movie in this country without being jumped on?" she asks in the opening of her lengthy defense of the film. Writing for *The New Yorker*, Kael calls *Bonnie and Clyde* an "excitingly American American movie" and notes that "the audience is alive to it." With almost eerie prescience, Kael enumerates the film's connections to the New Sentimentality: its deliberate blurring of the boundaries between high and low culture, its ambiguity, its appeals to the knowing spectator, and its ties to the French New Wave. The power of *Bonnie and Clyde*, Kael argues, is that it "brings into the almost frighteningly public world of movies things that people have been feeling and saying and writing about." Kael suggests that some of the backlash against the film may be the result of an "educated, or 'knowing' group" never again having "private possession" over elite sensibilities. "But even for that group," Kael notes, "there is an excitement in hearing its own private thoughts expressed out loud and in seeing something of its own sensibility become part of our common culture."[39]

A few years after the 1967 uproar over *Bonnie and Clyde*, the film critic Richard Schickel tried to make some sense out of the discursive devastation that had visited him and his colleagues. There had been press conferences, retractions, letters to the editor, even public fretting over manliness – all in print, and all precipitated by a single film. Kael emerged relatively unscathed. Others, including Schickel himself, had reversed their critical opinion after the tremendous popularity of the film had become painfully clear. As Schickel admitted in 1972, the film's "makers sensed far better than I the basic shift in the basic mood of its basically youthful audience." Making "two-bit mobsters into romantic outlaws – misunderstood, inarticulate, but sympathetic to other underdogs and irritants to authority (for which read 'the establishment')," *Bonnie and Clyde* had turned the *critical* establishment on its head. "By so doing," he noted with grudging admiration, "they created the first of the new cult films for the kids and helped establish the now infamous 'youth market.'" It was, in Schickel's words, "*the* major commercial discovery of the past five years, the largest single determinant of American film content in the late sixties and early seventies."[40] The discovery was not without a price, however. Schickel speculated that the *New York Times* critic Bosley Crowther had "hastened the end of his long career" by attacking *Bonnie and Clyde* three times in print.[41] Crowther's opinion had once meant something. After a barrage of letters from readers protesting Crowther's relentless criticism of *Bonnie and Clyde*, the *Times* summarily replaced him with Renata Adler, a twenty-six-year-old auteurist.

One could either love or hate *Bonnie and Clyde*, but Schickel's snideness notwithstanding, the film represented much more than simply the beginning of a new wave of "cult films for the kids." Its seeming allegiance to counterculture, its fragmented and stylized narrative, its not-so-subtle Freudian treatment of sexuality, and of course its graphic treatment of violence particularly threatened the dominant interpretive frames espoused by popular journalistic criticism. By asserting constructed notions of taste, relevance, audience, and authorship, the debate over

FIGURES 12 and 13

From "two-bit mobsters" to "romantic outlaws."

the film revealed powerful political and ideological subtexts. *Bonnie and Clyde* became the field upon which important struggles of subtext were waged – struggles between competing discourses of taste and relevance, struggles over the discursive legitimacy of established journalistic criticism, and struggles over a whole way of thinking and talking about the American audience.

This last-mentioned construct, the American audience, ultimately served as an incredibly important signifier in debates over the film. Yet it also remains something of a paradox. As Janet Staiger points out, the so-called reader of films often gets talked about in ways that are more fictive than actual.[42] This "fictive audience" is often that "other person" – that someone else who is, for example, incapable of resisting allegedly antisocial media influence. But fictive audiences do not materialize out of thin air. Like most fictions, the fictive audience for *Bonnie and Clyde* emerged out of a specific historical context. As subsequent debates attempted to construct this fictive audience for the film, discussion about this audience was helping the actual viewers and critics to help make sense of *Bonnie and Clyde*. This fiction, constructed within journalistic discourse, became its own text to be read, interpreted, fought over, and negotiated.

Invoking the fictive audience could establish discursive power and, by extension, ideological power. Just as some critics were threatened by the film's creation and recasting of gangster mythology – especially with regard to its effect on audiences – so too did critics fret over the perceived indifference of audiences who could no longer distinguish between good and bad, right and wrong, truth and falsity. Auteurism challenged this assumption. As Staiger notes, auteurism developed in popular criticism during the 1950s in response to an influx of post–World War II foreign films. The result of this reading strategy – looking at foreign films as the products of authors – helped differentiate these films from those made in Hollywood. This approach also helped differentiate the audiences attending these films.[43] In assuming that audiences wanted to see films as art, produced by a singular artistic vision, auteurism departed from more traditional discussions of motion pictures as an industrial art form. Thus auteurist approaches to *Bonnie and Clyde* could articulate the film's strategies in terms of both high art and a sophisticated audience.

As Staiger notes, positing authorship had long been a strategy used by the cultural elite and by well-educated audiences for reading *foreign* films, which were perceived as being more "realistic" and more "serious" and as having a "message." The message had to come from somewhere; the "author" was the logical choice.[44] Staiger traces such interpretive strategies to discussions of Italian neorealist films like *Open City* (1945), *Paisan* (1946), and the film that Bosley Crowther himself had defended – *The Miracle*.[45] Auteurism, by itself, was neither particularly novel nor particularly threatening. Attributing this interpretive practice to entertainment films, and by extension, to a mass audience capable of engaging in this activity, was what proved so menacing to popular journalistic criticism. For *Bonnie and Clyde*, authorship became part of the struggle to assert legitimacy for the film and its audience.

Popular criticism sought to strip *Bonnie and Clyde* of an auteurist reading, in part by asserting established notions of taste. John Simon objects to the film's self-conscious pretensions toward being a work of art, professing his belief that "true art is not aware of itself as art."[46] Yet such assertions are hardly made consistently. Crowther, who had condemned *Bonnie and Clyde* for its violence, could justify his praise for *Thunderball* (1965) because its excess violence was obviously lacking in seriousness.[47] Fredric Wertham, a critic of *Bonnie and Clyde* and a psychiatrist best known for his treatise on comic books, *Seduction of the Innocent*, argues that "under no circumstances was violent death . . . something to laugh about."[48]

Popular criticism also relied upon realist frames of reference to deny *Bonnie and Clyde* an auteurist reading. "In general," Wertham states, "it is a great fallacy to believe that in order to combat violence you have to show it as gorily as possible."[49]

Charles Champlin notes that *Bonnie and Clyde* had the capacity to "create the illusion of reality . . . so great that even the sophisticated viewer must surrender to the illusion." The critic could use his constructed notion of realism to validate his perspective. "Real violence on the screen," Champlin wrote, "is very real indeed. If it weren't, [fellow critics] Mr. Morgenstern, Mr. Crowther and the rest of us would have no cause to be concerned."[50]

Another strategy posited by popular criticism was that the auteurist-driven relevance of *Bonnie and Clyde* constituted nothing more than pandering to the audience. Crowther dismisses the depiction of Clyde's impotence as "a whiff of pornography."[51] He also objects to "excesses of visible violence," which he finds to be "deliberate pandering to an increasingly voracious public taste for blood and killing."[52] Writing for the *New American Review*, Stanley Kauffman objects to the popularization of previously elite culture. He blames the auteurist sensibilities of films like *Bonnie and Clyde* in part upon "the ravenous appetite of the new middle class for culture-status."[53] But "college-bred" industry personnel are also partly to blame, having "nicely adjusted their ambitions for intellectual prestige" to "intense commercial pressure."[54] Kauffman's assault upon this "ravenous appetite" was in keeping with the cultural traditionalism of the *New American Review*. The editors of this annual claimed not to "whore after the young and the wild or to publish material merely because its like has never before been seen on land or sea," professing a belief that "the cultural tradition needs to be restated, not abandoned."[55]

Such restatements, of course, have powerful ideological implications. A common objection to *Bonnie and Clyde* faulted its lack of what critics called historical reality. Both Kauffman and Crowther object to the way in which the story's "facts" have been altered. Crowther protests making "mean, ugly, sexually maladjusted roughnecks" into "free-wheeling, fun-loving kids, as handsome and artificially charming as Warren Beatty and Faye Dunaway" because this was "a dangerous distortion" of both "facts" and "plausibility."[56] Interestingly, Kauffman decries auteurism while blaming Penn's authorship for the story's divergence from reality. In Crowther's eyes, *Bonnie and Clyde* assumed no responsibility as "authentic biography or social history, instead serving as a clever and effective distortion."[57] Kauffman could have forgiven as "dramatic license" the fact that "in reality" Bonnie was "ugly" and an adulterer and that she "continued to have a busy sex life of an eccentric kind" even after she met Clyde. The objection to relevance barely conceals the hostility of heterosexist propriety toward changes that Kauffman finds aggrandizing and "hollow." Especially galling to him are the film's Freudian symbolism and its "economic determinism." Kauffman is at once shocked by the film's overt displays of sexuality ("the clearest suggestion of fellatio that I have seen in an American film") and dismissive of its "new intellectual veneer."[58]

Kauffman prefers a politically conservative veneer. Throughout his review, he uses thinly cloaked anti-Communist rhetoric to dismiss the film. He notes how "the dispossessed treat the wounded bandits like People's Heroes." He compares the film to "thirties propaganda plays" of striking workers leading "happy, if harried" home lives.[59] Kauffman's biases become even more pronounced when he attacks what he calls the proletarian theme of the film, using "proletarian" interchangeably with "economic determinism." The police shown in the movie, Kauffman notes:

> are usually poor men, too, and that – in those Depression days – they felt very lucky to have jobs and would do almost anything to keep them. (So would any of those dispossessed farmers, if they had been able to get police jobs). Clyde never kills anyone until a grocer whom he is robbing tries to kill him. This shocks Clyde – the discovery that people will kill to protect their property.

By the violent climax of the film, Kauffman argues, the audience has no sympathy for the heroes, because this sympathy "has been dissipated by the dozens of other victims of society – who happened to be tellers or policemen – already killed by the Barrow gang." Kauffman is, of course, naturalizing the workings of the dominant here. There is no power differential between state and citizen; the police are just folks doing their jobs. Class conflict is obliterated; even the dispossessed farmer would willingly become a representative of the state when hardened deviants come to town.[60]

Despite these and other protests against auteurist readings of *Bonnie and Clyde*, auteurism was in fact highly compatible with dominant discursive practice. As mentioned earlier, many popular critics were already using this approach with foreign films. Andrew Sarris had articulated auteurism with particularly nationalist and militaristic inflections. Danae Clark has shown that auteurism effectively conceals capitalist demands upon the rank-and-file labor force (the technicians) to be efficient, thus naturalizing the entire process, and gives studios greater power to differentiate their product and to control labor with pay incentives and large budgets. "Auteur criticism can thus be read," she writes, "as an attempt to restore the virtues of art to a system of productivity designed to minimize creative difference and individual accomplishment."[61]

Since popular criticism had already employed authorship as a strategy in reading foreign films, and since auteurism could actually serve the ideological needs of the dominant, auteurism in and of itself was not the threat. Instead, popular criticism objected to the way in which auteurism could at once fragment the general audience for entertainment films and popularize the marginal. Jay Emanuel, the publisher of *The Motion Picture Exhibitor*, laments the days when "excessive screen violence and sadism were confined to fast-buck films designed for strictly limited playoff." As Emanuel suggests, part of what made films like *Bonnie and Clyde* so shocking was that they were no longer relegated to fringe producers, distributors, and exhibitors. In his view, "Films no longer cater to mainstream tastes; theaters have ceased to help audiences choose the kinds of films they wish to see." Instead, the product differentiates itself for consumers.

"Top stars and top directors used to bring in big audiences automatically," Emanuel writes. "Today, however, audiences shop for their entertainment as carefully as they shop for their clothes."[62]

This fragmented, consumer audience for *Bonnie and Clyde* could still fulfill a variety of economic and ideological functions. When Warner Brothers–Seven Arts re-released the film, it was shown in "prestige" engagements. The film influenced European designers, who in turn influenced American designers into bringing back hats and caps, wide lapels, wide ties, stripes, and colored suits.[63] David Newman and Robert Benton celebrated the film's phenomenal influence and popularity – what they called catching "lightning in a bottle."[64] But although a fragmented audience of consumers could still fulfill certain aspects of capitalism, popular criticism remained in crisis over how to explain *Bonnie and Clyde*'s immense popularity.

As a result of the controversy over *Bonnie and Clyde*, critics and audiences began to talk about a youth audience in new ways. This construction could help explain the film's enormous popularity. Potentially threatening, the youth audience could also function as consumers, thus helping repair the discursive ruptures that controversy over the film had suggested. As Aniko Bodroghkozy suggests, the visible traces left by the rebellious youth movement of the 1960s were produced by young white middle-, upper-middle-, and upper-class males who could align themselves with some aspects of the counterculture while actively working against the interests of marginalized groups, such as women.[65] That a Hollywood movie like *Bonnie and Clyde* could appeal to rebellious youth served at least two important functions: first, it meant that the potency of films in reaching marginalized audiences was solidified; and second, it meant that the youth audience could be contextualized within mainstream culture, tethering this audience to the film's success – and therefore resolving the threat of otherwise alienated readers.

Instead of addressing the possibility of multiple or serious readings of so-called entertainment films, popular discourse on

Bonnie and Clyde promoted this new fictive youth audience. Bosley Crowther explains that the film was calculated to "gratify the preconceptions and illusions of young people who had come of age with the Beatles and Bob Dylan, the philosophy of doing-your-thing and the notion that defying the Establishment was beautiful and brave." He ultimately finds the film to be "clever" in capturing "the amoral restlessness of youth in those years."[66] Richard Schickel expresses amazement that he and his fellow critics did not initially see how *Bonnie and Clyde* had "plugged into youth's new, or at least newly intense, image of itself as a band of outsiders entitled to embrace (or at least applaud) even illegal methods in attacking the corrupt, corrupting social order ruled by old men and institutions."[67] Even the film's defenders acceded to this new discursive audience text. "Youth identified with *Bonnie and Clyde*," one book explains, "because of their [the protagonists'] plight – two small people caught up in 'the system.' "[68] One law student, responding to Crowther's missives, argues for the "special relevance" of *Bonnie and Clyde* to "a generation seeking to bring new and real meaning to life in a decade characterized by brutal, senseless violence."[69] John Baxter interprets spectators for *Bonnie and Clyde* as "young audiences [who] saw Penn's couple as saints for a disenchanted age" because everything else in a "society devoid of social purpose" was unworthy of "emulation."[70]

The most powerful feature of this discussion was the way in which it ultimately eviscerated the possibility of resistance. Instead, it rendered the youth audience an elusive component of consumer culture. As Bodroghkozy notes, common wisdom dictated that when the industry went looking for a hit with youth audiences, it failed. But the films that the industry expected to flop, like *Bonnie and Clyde* and *The Graduate* (1967), turned out to be wildly popular with young audiences.[71] Popular discourse could have repaired the rupture these films presented by depicting the youth audience as powerful, untapped, and unpredictable, but an entity that could nonetheless function as consumers. By articulating concepts of relevance, taste, and auteurism,

FIGURES 14 and 15
Capturing "lightning in a bottle": *Bonnie and Clyde*'s wardrobe influenced clothing styles for years to come.

popular discourse was able to make sense of the unfamiliar fictive audience it had created. As a critic for *See Magazine* noted,
Bonnie and Clyde and *The Graduate* represented a turning point
for films. But it was a turning point that could be explained only
in terms of a youth audience able to generate "colossal remuner-
ation" for "films of high artistic achievement."[72]

By the time Warner Brothers released Oliver Stone's *Natural
Born Killers* in 1994, both the youth audience and their emergent
position as "knowing" spectators had become thoroughly com-
modified. The distribution company for *Bonnie and Clyde* of the
1960s, which had struggled to retool itself after the breakup of
the studio system in the 1940s, now belonged to one of a handful of media conglomerates – Time Warner – whose holdings
include Turner Broadcasting, HBO, cable systems, magazines,
records, comic books, book publishing, and theme parks. In the
summer of 1967, amid the riots and rebellions, Warner Brothers
could release a movie that basically said "fucking cops!" In the
summer of 1994, Warner Brothers could release a movie that
basically said "fucking media!" By that time, Rodney King had
become a dim cultural memory, and L.A. was arguably just a
"riot, not rebellion."

NOTES

This work was supported by a Purdue Research Foundation Summer
    Faculty Grant. I am indebted to The Indiana University–Purdue Uni-
    versity Fort Wayne Documentary Delivery Service for their indispen-
    sable work. Many thanks to Frank Beaver, Glenn Man, Nancy Virtue,
    and Les Friedman for their insightful comments. Any shortcomings
    herein exist in spite of their input.

1. Dole, "Remarks," 102.
2. Ibid., 103.
3. See, e.g., Roger Ebert, review of *Natural Born Killers* (1994), *Cine-
    mania '96*, CD-ROM.
4. Todd Gitlin, *The Whole World Is Watching*, 199.
5. Insightful discussions with Nancy Virtue helped a great deal in
    clarifying these thoughts on the movie.
6. Fiske, *Media Matters*, 1.

7. "Human Rights and Social Justice, 1967," *The People's Chronology* (1994), *Microsoft Bookshelf '95*, CD-ROM.
8. "Political Events, 1967," *People's Chronology, Microsoft Bookshelf '95*, CD-ROM.
9. "Human Rights," *People's Chronology, Microsoft Bookshelf '95*, CD-ROM.
10. Ibid.
11. Man, *Radical Visions*, 2.
12. Beaver, *Bosley Crowther*, 74.
13. Ruth A. Inglis, "Self-Regulation in Operation," 380–1. Unless otherwise noted, all emphasis appears in the original source.
14. Beaver, *Bosley Crowther*, 78.
15. Zuker, *Arthur Penn*, 3.
16. Duberman, *Black Mountain*, 260–4.
17. Zuker, *Arthur Penn*, 5, 168.
18. Barnouw, *Tube of Plenty*, 273–4.
19. Newman and Benton, "The New Sentimentality," 25–31.
20. Ibid., 25.
21. Alpert, "Crime Wave," 40.
22. Daku, review of *Bonnie and Clyde*, 6.
23. Crowther, "Shoot-Em-Up Film Opens World Fete," 32.
24. Ibid.
25. Ibid.
26. Ibid.
27. Carroll, "Bonnie and Clyde Brutal and Brilliant," 44.
28. Winsten, "Bonnie and Clyde in Dual Bow," 28.
29. Morgenstern, "Two for a Tommy Gun," 65; "Low-Down Hoe-Down," 78.
30. Crowther, "Screen: Bonnie and Clyde Arrives," 36.
31. Gilliatt, "The Party," 77–79.
32. Sarris, "Films," 21.
33. "Bonnie, Clyde," sec. 2, 11+.
34. Teresa Hayden, "The 'Have-Nots,' " letter to the editor, *New York Times*, 27 August 1967, 20.
35. Arthur Penn, "The Arthur Penn Interview," *Cahiers du Cinéma* (December 1967) in *Bonnie and Clyde*, comp. and ed. Wake and Hayden, 173.
36. Morella and Epstein, *Rebels*, 163–4.
37. "Bonnie and Clyde Building in N.Y.," 4.
38. "Smash-Hit Killers," 23.
39. Kael, "Bonnie and Clyde," 147.
40. Schickel, *Second Sight*, 143.

41. Ibid.
42. Staiger, *Interpreting Films*, xi.
43. Ibid., 178.
44. Ibid., 181–82.
45. Ibid., 188.
46. Simon, *Movies into Film*, 163.
47. Beaver, *Bosley Crowther*, 161–2.
48. Wertham, "Is So Much Violence in Films Necessary?" 4.
49. Ibid.
50. Champlin, "Violence and the Film Critic," 30.
51. Crowther, *Reruns*, 201.
52. Ibid., 200.
53. Kauffman, "Looking at Films," 162.
54. Ibid., 161–2.
55. Solatoroff, introduction, n.p.
56. Crowther, *Reruns*, 200.
57. Ibid., 203–4.
58. Kauffman, "Looking at Films," 159–60.
59. Ibid., 160.
60. Ibid., 160–1.
61. Clark, *Negotiating Hollywood*, 6–7.
62. Emanuel, "What Price Screen Violence?" 37.
63. Morella and Epstein, *Rebels*, 164–5.
64. David Newman and Robert Benton, "Lightning in a Bottle," in *Bonnie and Clyde,* comp. and ed. Wake and Hayden, 13.
65. Bodroghkozy, "Groove Tube and Reel Revolution," 19–29.
66. Crowther, *Reruns*, 203–4.
67. Schickel, *Second Sight*, 143–4.
68. Morella and Epstein, *Rebels*, 165.
69. Stephen M. Ege, letter to the editor, *New York Times*, in Savary and Carrico, *Contemporary Film*, 35.
70. Baxter, *Hollywood in the Sixties*, 35.
71. Bodroghkozy, "Groove Tube and Reel Revolution," 119–29.
72. Sal Giarrizzo, in Savary and Carrico, *Contemporary Film*, 24.

WORKS CITED

Alpert, Hollis. "Crime Wave." *Saturday Review*, 5 August 1967, 40.
Barnouw, Erik. *Tube of Plenty: The Evolution of American Television*. Rev. ed. Oxford: Oxford University Press, 1982.
Baxter, John. *Hollywood in the Sixties*. The International Film Guide Series. London: Tantivy Press; New York: Barnes, 1972.

Beaver, Frank Eugene. *Bosley Crowther: Social Critic of the Film, 1940–1967*. Ph.D. diss., University of Michigan, 1970. Dissertations on Films Series. Arno Press Cinema Program. New York: Arno Press, 1974.

Bodroghkozy, Aniko. "Groove Tube and Reel Revolution: The Youth Rebellions of the 1960s and Popular Culture." Ph.D. diss., University of Wisconsin-Madison, 1994.

"Bonnie, Clyde." Letters to the editor. *New York Times*, 27 August 1967, sec. 2, 11+.

"Bonnie and Clyde Building in N.Y." *Variety*, 13 September 1967, 4.

Carroll, Kathleen. "Bonnie and Clyde Brutal and Brilliant." Review of *Bonnie and Clyde*. *Daily News*, 14 August 1967, late edition, 44.

Champlin, Charles. "Violence and the Film Critic." *Journal of the Producers Guild of America*, 9.4 (1967): 29–30.

Cinemania '96. CD-ROM. Redmond, WA: Microsoft, 1995.

Clark, Danae. *Negotiating Hollywood: The Cultural Politics of Actors' Labor*. Minneapolis: University of Minnesota Press, 1995.

Crowther, Bosley. *Reruns: Fifty Memorable Films*. New York: Putnam, 1978.

——. "Screen: Bonnie and Clyde Arrives." Review of *Bonnie and Clyde*. *New York Times*, 14 August 1967, 36.

——. "Shoot-Em-Up Film Opens World Fete." *New York Times*, 7 August 1967, 32.

Daku. Review of *Bonnie and Clyde*. *Variety*, 9 August 1967, 6.

Dole, Bob. "Remarks by Senator Bob Dole." Speech prepared for the 1996 Presidential Campaign, Los Angeles, CA, 31 May 1995. Reprinted in *Taking Sides: Clashing Views on Controversial Issues in Mass Media and Society*, edited by Alison Alexander and Jarice Hanson, 102–5. 4th ed. Guilford, CT: Dushkin/Brown, Benchmark, 1997.

Duberman, Martin. *Black Mountain: An Exploration in Community*. Garden City, NY: Anchor-Doubleday, 1973.

Emanuel, Jay. "What Price Screen Violence?" *Journal of the Producers Guild of America* 9.4 (1967): 37.

Fiske, John. *Media Matters: Race and Gender in U.S. Politics*. Rev. ed. Minneapolis: University of Minnesota Press, 1996.

Gilliatt, Penelope. "The Party." Review of *Bonnie and Clyde*. *The New Yorker*, 19 August 1967, 77–79.

Gitlin, Todd. *The Whole World Is Watching: Mass Media in the Making and Unmaking of the New Left*. Berkeley: University of California Press, 1980.

Inglis, Ruth A. "Self-Regulation in Operation." *The American Film Indus-*

try, edited by Tino Balio, 377–400. Rev. ed. Madison: University of Wisconsin Press, 1985.

Kael, Pauline. "Bonnie and Clyde." Review of *Bonnie and Clyde*. *The New Yorker*, 21 October 1967, 147–71.

Kauffman, Stanley. "Looking at Films." *New American Review* 2 (1968): 159–60.

"Low-Down Hoe-Down." Review of *Bonnie and Clyde*. *Time*, 25 August 1967, 78.

Man, Glenn. *Radical Visions: American Film Renaissance, 1967–1976*. Contributions to the Study of Popular Culture 41. Westport, CT: Greenwood Press, 1994.

Microsoft Bookshelf '95. CD-ROM. Redmond, WA: Microsoft, 1995.

Morella, Joe, and Edward Z. Epstein. *Rebels: The Rebel Hero in Films*. Secaucus, NJ: Citadel Press, 1971.

Morgenstern, Joseph. "Two for a Tommy Gun." Review of *Bonnie and Clyde*. *Newsweek*, 21 August 1967, 65.

Newman, David, and Robert Benton. "The New Sentimentality." *Esquire* 62 (July 1964): 25–31.

Sarris, Andrew. "Films." Review of *Bonnie and Clyde*. *Village Voice*, 24 August 1967, 21.

Savary, Louis M., and J. Paul Carrico, eds. *Contemporary Film and the New Generation*. Youth World. New York: Association Press, 1971.

Schickel, Richard. *Second Sight: Notes on Some Movies, 1965–1970*. New York: Simon and Schuster, 1972.

Simon, John. *Movies into Film: Film Criticism, 1967–1970*. New York: Delta-Dell, 1971.

"Smash-Hit Killers." *Observer*, 8 October 1967, 23.

Solatoroff, Theodore. Introduction. *New American Review* 2 (1968): n.p.

Staiger, Janet. *Interpreting Films: Studies in the Historical Reception of American Cinema*. Princeton: Princeton University Press, 1992.

Wake, Sandra, and Nicola Hayden, comps. and eds. *Bonnie and Clyde*. New York: Lorrimer, 1972.

Wertham, Fredric. "Is So Much Violence in Films Necessary?" *Journal of the Producers Guild of America* 9.4 (1967): 4.

Winsten, Archer. "Bonnie and Clyde in Dual Bow – Tale of Bad-Boy and His Moll." Review of *Bonnie and Clyde*. *New York Post*, 14 August 1967, final edition, 28.

Zuker, Joel S. *Arthur Penn: A Guide to References and Resources*. Boston: G. K. Hall and, Co., 1980.

Model Criminals

VISUAL STYLE IN *BONNIE AND CLYDE*

The first five shots of *Bonnie and Clyde* comprise one of the most daring and jarring opening sequences in American film history. Dissolving from a photo of Clyde Barrow (Warren Beatty), we see an extreme close-up of Bonnie (Faye Dunaway), specifically her mouth, as she finishes applying lipstick. As the camera quickly pans with her appraising look in her mirror and draws back, bright light conveys the stifling heat in Bonnie's room. An industrial machine in the neighborhood throbs in a steady, dull beat. Bonnie gets up, crosses the room to flop on her bed, and pounds on the headrail. The low-angle shot of Bonnie reveals the drab walls and ceiling of her room. The camera rises and dollies in on her eyes for another extreme close-up after she punches the bedpost. Bonnie then looks over the rail, gets up again, and crosses the room to get dressed reluctantly. She appears to us a restless, potentially ferocious, caged being (a metaphor encouraged by the birdcage just visible in the back corner).

One of the many pleasures of viewing *Bonnie and Clyde* resides in appreciating how much of the film's density and complexity can be related back to this opening scene. The immediacy of this sequence is part of its boldness; through extremely close shots, it binds the viewer to Bonnie's predicament, inaugurating the intense identification of audience with character that distinguishes this film.[1] These first few shots also underline Bonnie's sexuality (not only her nakedness, but her narcissism) as a primary element of her character and her discontent. When we subsequently see her from Clyde's point of view in the front yard, Bonnie's full-length, naked appearance in the window similarly conveys this sense of vitality bursting at the seams of domestic entrapment.

Such images and Bonnie's actions imply that her dissatisfaction will generate many of the events that follow. It certainly impels her into a frenzy of motion: when she spots Clyde, she tells him to wait and, after having shifted about and dressed as slowly as possible, she now hurriedly throws on her dress and pours down the stairs to confront him. The motif of Bonnie's imprisonment reappears constantly, as she, Clyde, C. W. Moss (Michael J. Pollard), Buck Barrow (Gene Hackman), and Blanche Barrow (Estelle Parsons) are driving endlessly in stolen cars or retiring in depressing motel rooms;[2] the entire gang experiences this sense of confinement, but no one feels it as keenly as Bonnie and, by extension, the viewer. In fact, during the noisy checkers game in Joplin between C. W. and Buck Barrow, Bonnie starts pacing impatiently with swirling hair, and Penn photographs her with a slightly low angle identical to that used in her West Dallas bedroom. Bonnie has not escaped her initial predicament.

In addition, beginning with Bonnie's very first view of Clyde from her room, everyone in this film will be introduced, perceived, misunderstood, rejected, explained, and destroyed through house and car windows – up to the very last shot, where we see the triumphant Sheriff Hamer through the rear windshield of the couple's car.[3] Windows convey the characters' confinement and limitations – psychological and physical – throughout the film.

There are two other, equally compelling but usually unremarked features of the very first scene in the film: its uncommunicativeness and its abrupt editing scheme. Whereas *Bonnie and Clyde* typically lets the audience know what it needs to know for the story to proceed, here the viewer relies on what is shown, not what is said, to interpret the scene. Recognizable as Bonnie's frustration might be, there is no dialogue to confirm it: she could be the heroine of a gothic thriller, a woman in the attic, rather than the heroine of a crime-spree saga. Viewers attempt, in Robert Kolker's words, "to make sense of who and what Bonnie is," and they do not have much time before Clyde is introduced.[4] It is not until several scenes later that Clyde articulates the curse of Bonnie's quotidian despair ("And now you wake up every morning and you hate it. You just hate it. . . . So you go on home and you sit in your room and you think, now when . . . and how . . . am I ever gonna get away from this?") that we have previously observed.[5] So the film's narration shifts gears, from a total immersion in a visual connection with Bonnie's physical presence, to a purely verbal interpretation of what we have seen. Clyde's perceptiveness, however incredible, is a gift to the viewer.

The abrupt editing of the opening scene previews the dazzling visual fireworks to come.[6] The camera swiftly pans right from the extreme close-up on Bonnie's lips to a medium shot of her face reflected in a mirror. After this, each of the next three shots is joined by discontinuous cuts. Bonnie starts to turn right in the earlier shot; she is up and has almost completed the turn at the start of the next (Figs. 16 and 17). From a low-angle view of Bonnie lowering herself onto the bed, Penn and the film's editor Dede Allen cut to a shot of Bonnie's already falling onto the mattress (Figs. 18 and 19). After she pounds the bedpost, she moves to get up, and the frame is full of her long hair; the next shot shows her fully upright, her naked back to the camera as she strides to a screen where she will begin dressing.

These uneasy shot transitions give Bonnie's frustration a visual and temporal frisson. If these are not the jump cuts of Jean-Luc Godard's *Breathless* (1959), they nonetheless violate the general principles of traditional continuity editing. One can read these cuts as a visualization of Bonnie's despair at her existence; Arthur Penn has described their logic as "a kind of metaphor:"

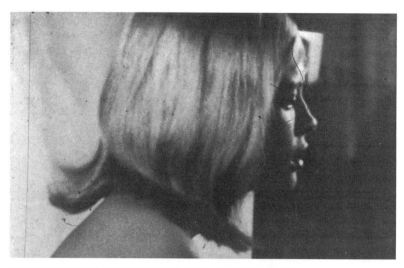

FIGURES 16 and 17

The first example of discontinuous editing: the last frame of the first shot of Bonnie and the first frame of the second show a jump in her position as she turns to get up from her vanity mirror.

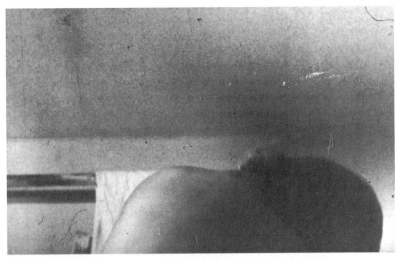

FIGURES 18 and 19
Abrupt editing continues in the second cut of the film: Bonnie barely begins to lower herself onto the bed in the second shot and quickly lands on it in the third.

I was not interested in continuity of action. I was interested in the idea of appetite – I had to establish the appetite of this woman for anything that would replace the tedium of her life. So that's how we developed it from that close-up on her mouth. And that set the tone for the whole film. With the editing, we wanted nervous bursts of energy, a way of showing how Bonnie felt. It was a metaphoric visual style.[7]

Significantly, discontinuous cuts appear again in more subtle ways throughout the film, but they return with a vengeance in the final ambush, just as the hints of violence in Bonnie's abrupt gestures will gradually escalate across the film.[8] It is as if Clyde's appearance in Bonnie's front yard quells not only Bonnie's frustrated funk but also the film's proliferating visual tension, shot by shot, in that opening scene.

The foregoing analysis should suggest some of *Bonnie and Clyde*'s intricate architecture. To watch *Bonnie and Clyde* three decades after its premiere is to be struck by the film's emotional generosity toward its characters, its unflagging sense of the gangster's existential absurdity, and equally, its visual panache. Reviewers noted from the outset how the film continually throws the spectator off guard – and not just because of the sporadic outbursts of violence that confound its conception of Bonnie and Clyde as engaging, glamorous, overgrown children. The film's fusion of American and European "art" filmmaking was another source of spectator disorientation, albeit one Arthur Penn had previously explored in *Mickey One* (1964). Although critics and devotees of the film have acknowledged *Bonnie and Clyde*'s complex, hybrid visual style from its premiere until the present day, it has never been documented with the benefit of a close analysis. To do so is my primary aim in this essay.

First, as Arthur Penn's earlier comments suggest, the film's visual style is closely linked to Bonnie and Clyde's personal traits, their quirks of personality. Visual style is also, as always, a vehicle for the film's narration. Before considering visual style proper (editing, camerawork, and mise-en-scène), it is worth pausing over the gang members' characterizations and the way the film conveys information to the audience.

Bonnie and Clyde's varied film style is related to the contradictory traits of the gang members in the script. The script opposes Bonnie and Clyde against unusually comical representatives of conventional morality: Blanche Barrow, a hypocritical, self-absorbed "hausfrau" (in the screenwriters David Newman and Robert Benton's terms), who is outraged by the gang's conduct but demands a share of the take; Ivan Moss (Dub Taylor), whose obsession with his son C. W.'s chest tattoo outweighs any moral qualms about C. W.'s lawlessness or choice of friends; and the gang's nemesis, Frank Hamer (Denver Pyle), an impassive, cold-blooded bounty hunter who has no moral claim on defending the law.

Bonnie and Clyde's combination of amorality and childlike innocence is the major paradox in the film, and the one most closely keyed to the film's visual style; but they also display other traits worth noting. Clyde has acute insight into people's circumstances (he "knows" Bonnie's, C. W.'s, and Sheriff Hamer's histories when he first meets them), but he is utterly oblivious to their thoughts. He cannot, for example, understand why a butcher would want to kill a robber, or why Bonnie is upset with his regret over the gang's impractical bankrobbing routine rather than over their outlaw life, as they recuperate in the Moss home. Bonnie's style consciousness (and repeated mirror checks) makes her a fashion plate (with or without a cigar in her mouth), yet she remains rooted in her poor southern milieu and is perfectly comfortable with the earthy, burping, C. W., who is given to lounging around in his underwear.

Regarding Bonnie, John Cawelti has argued persuasively that hers is the primary consciousness of *Bonnie and Clyde*:

> Bonnie is the true protagonist of the film; it is her sense of frustration and entrapment that appears at the very beginning; it is her response to Clyde's fantasy of wealth and power that creates the Barrow gang. It is she who decides to stay with Clyde. . . . In many ways, then, the film is structured around the series of decisions and actions that lead Bonnie from her

tawdry bedroom to a terrible death, along with the growing
awareness and realization that this movement involves. . . .
Her increasing awareness and depth, in contrast to the comic
limitations of the other characters, make her the true center of
the film.[9]

Truly, Bonnie provides the emotional core of the film, for all the
reasons that Cawelti enumerates, and more. One measure of
Bonnie's growth is her changing reaction to Clyde's impotence,
from her initial humiliation and indignation to a comprehend-
ing sensitivity;[10] another would be the shift from her insensitive
absorption in *The Gold Diggers of 1933* after Clyde has killed his
first victim to her broadening awareness of the pathos of their
lives.

Yet the play of point of view in *Bonnie and Clyde* is quite
complex. Most dramatically, the film's optical perspective shifts
away from Bonnie to Clyde early on. In the first few minutes,
Bonnie's view predominates. We see Clyde beside her mother's
car before Bonnie does, but much of the scene's byplay turns on
Bonnie's discovery of Clyde, shown from her vantage point at
the second-story window. When they go for a Coke, we see
Clyde first, from Bonnie's point of view – his life of crime makes
him fascinating to her. We do not enter the grocery store in
West Dallas with Clyde, but remain on the street with Bonnie
(Fig. 20). As we will see, the visual treatment of their initial
flirtation casts them as equals: in terms of shot composition and
editing, of movement within and out of the frame, Bonnie's
taunting of Clyde as a coward and her repulsion at his sexual
impotence are presented in the same, evenhanded seesaw fashion, using extensive shot–reverse shot editing.

Beginning with the roadhouse meal, however, Clyde's point
of view predominates. In fact, his very first line of dialogue
inside the cafe comes as a virtual reply to a question Bonnie had
started to ask at the end of the previous scene. His look at the
waitress motivates his directive on Bonnie's hairstyle (his per-
emptory command to "change that," to eliminate her spit curl).
Bonnie has been sassy and defiant, as she is when Clyde first

FIGURE 20
Early, the film's point of view remains clearly aligned with Bonnie.

meets her; but once Clyde has proven himself by robbing the West Dallas store and by proposing fantasies of wealth and fame, she subordinates her independence to his authority. At the mortgaged farmhouse the next day, though we awaken with Bonnie, once Clyde shows up we see whatever he looks at – the farmer, his truck, his family, his fieldhand, the weathervane, the shattered windows – point-of-view editing cues us to follow Clyde's perceptions as they occur. In contrast to the first (grocery store) robbery where Clyde "proves" he has the guts to use a gun, in the second robbery attempt, the camera anticipates Clyde's entry into the defaulted bank, by shooting his entrance from *inside* the bank and (intercut with shots of Bonnie waiting in the car) offering us hand-held shots that survey the bank from his nervous viewpoint.

Henceforth, in scenes where Bonnie and Clyde exchange knowing looks, Penn employs shot–reverse shot editing to suggest their partnership. This is one signaling device to demonstrate the strengthening bond between them – the assortment of quick gestures and glances that demonstrate their growing relationship. Clyde taps Bonnie's thigh in giddy excitement when Davis, the black fieldhand, is about to fire Clyde's gun at the mortgaged farmhouse; Bonnie is appalled that Clyde would tell the farmer they rob banks but smiles in response to his decisive nod, and it is she who repeats the phrase when they introduce themselves to C. W. Moss. In fact, by the time they meet up with C. W., they communicate through an extensive code of quizzical looks and gestures as they determine whether or not to invite C. W. to join them (Fig. 21). They employ this system repeatedly, as when they settle into the first motel with Buck and Blanche, or as they exchange gleeful looks while dining on hamburgers with Eugene (Gene Wilder) and Velma (Evans Evans). These looks and gestures, as much as the uncontrollable getaways, give the couple the "underlying aliveness, an innate sensitiveness of response" that Robin Wood describes.[11] Their visual communication culminates in the final ambush: when Clyde realizes something is up, he is shot turning around and jumping into the frame to face Bonnie; they exchange looks of affection (Bonnie in progressively closer shots) before the shooting starts, a final, intimate affirmation of their love.[12]

There will be scenes in which a new character's point of view temporarily prevails – as when Blanche first meets the gang; there will be scenes in which Penn favors no character through camera framing. But if anyone's point of view predominates in a given scene, and if any character's vision is decisive, it is usually Clyde's: he is the first to see "the laws" and Frank Hamer in Missouri, and he senses the fatal ambush, albeit too late. Passing the film's visual authority from Bonnie to Clyde counters the prior introduction of Clyde's impotence; along with his willingness to use a gun, which is shown to be compensation for his sexual dysfunction, Clyde asserts leadership over Bonnie and the gang with an authority that Penn's shot-by-shot construction of scenes reinforces.

Bonnie's optical point of view prevails in two exceptional

FIGURE 21
Bonnie and Clyde develop an extensive code of nonverbal communication through looks and gestures.

sequences. When she reads "The Ballad of Bonnie and Clyde,"
the poem that in Cawelti's words frees "her lover from his impotent anonymity by embodying his fantasy of fame in
words,"[13] the film cuts to the poem's publication in the newspaper and then to a shot of Hamer reading it, before coming
back to Bonnie. But this segment is localized, isolated from the
film's regime of vision, and embedded in the romantic relationship between the gangsters, which the film delicately delineates
as a traditional, male-dominated couple. Similarly, the Parker
family reunion sequence can be seen as the one extended lapse
into subjectivity in the entire film. The pronounced emotional
tone arising from the gauzy filters and backlighting creates an
enveloping, comforting haze. Along with the use of slow motion
as a nephew slides down a hill and the reduced sound level, such
stylization marks the reunion as someone's (or the group's) subjective perception of the event – but it is never clearly marked as
Bonnie's.

Thus, Clyde and Bonnie's point of view dominates the film, while their violent amorality and tender naïveté constitute the film's major paradox. Appropriately, *Bonnie and Clyde*'s eclectic stylistic fireworks, from long takes to rapid editing, from carefully edited dialogue scenes to discontinuous cuts, bespeak a free-form approach to film style that marvelously visualizes the couple's unconventionality and conveys character experience with maximum intensity.

There is, for example, the film's alternation of frenzied movement and absolute stillness, between the robberies and shootouts on the one hand, and the quiet domestic scenes on the other.[14] The latter include one-shot scenes and long takes in intimate settings, such as Buck's first telling of the "Don't sell that cow!" joke, in which the camera simply dollies into a medium (process) shot of the two Barrow brothers driving to Joplin. Another one-shot scene takes place in the motel when Bonnie hovers over the apparently sleeping Clyde during their first night with C. W. This early shot is repeated late in the film when Clyde tells Bonnie what he "would do differently" with the gang. Her disappointment at his focus on the mechanics of their life of crime, rather than on their unthinking rejection of domestic stability, leads Bonnie to lie in bed unresponsively while Clyde hovers over *her*, as a reply to the earlier shot (Fig. 22). Other longer takes appear in the desolate shots of Bonnie and Clyde in a hotel room when Clyde has failed to make love to Bonnie after his first killing. Although such drab interiors may resemble Bonnie's bedroom,[15] visually suggesting how little has changed for her, the duration of such shots could not contrast more with the jagged editing of that opening scene in Bonnie's room, or with the frenetic montage that occurs during the various gun battles and the final assault.

So often during the film, rapidly edited bank robberies or shootouts are followed by longer shots of the gang making their getaway. Such a contrast of visual techniques culminates in the film's final seconds. After the multicamera, multispeed, multiangle montage of Clyde and Bonnie's annihilation, five shots show

FIGURE 22
An example of Penn's one-shot takes that express complicated
emotional relationships.

the killers and onlookers tentatively emerging from their hiding
places. The final, twenty-five-second shot looks through an open
car window (the driver's side door), as the black farmers edge
forward and Mr. Moss comes out from his truck. The camera
dollies past countless bullet holes to the back of the aerated car,
where it looks through the rear window. From this angle, Hamer
and his deputies are visible, examining their handiwork – their
eyelines trace an itinerary from, first, Bonnie's corpse in the
driver's seat and then Clyde's (both below the frame line of the
shot), before letting their machine guns drop, and the everpre-
sent trees are visible in the rear window's reflection (Fig. 23).

Like the film's opening sequence, this remarkable shot com-
bines various motifs that have informed the entire film: the
prevalence of rural landscapes that connote both the dreariness
of impoverished lives and the potential for freedom; the con-
stricted visions and viewpoints of characters who live on the
run and on the road, who contend with the advantages and

limitations of mobile domesticity (the car as a dining room when they eat hamburgers with Velma and Eugene; the car as recovery room after the ambush in which Buck is fatally shot). When the gang captured Hamer, we saw him, his nose pressed to the rear window of a car, from the back seat. Now, at the conclusion of this elaborate shot, we see him from a reverse angle, looking down at his former tormentors.

For all of *Bonnie and Clyde*'s stylistic variety, however, the film's editing and pacing are its distinguishing features. We may think of Sergei Eisenstein's *Potemkin* (1925) when the bank teller is shot in the face or Godard's *Breathless* when Penn uses abrupt cuts, but *Bonnie and Clyde* more typically demonstrates a penchant for slicing space and time into fragments and assembling them for the greatest impact on the spectator (in accordance with the prescriptions of Eisenstein's contemporary, V. I. Pudovkin). The building up of scenes out of quickly edited shots begins with the credit sequence; the ambush sequences in Joplin, Platte City, and Dexter pick up and extend the intense fragmentation of space and time that marked the film's opening scene in Bonnie's room, increasing the pace of cuts with each attack. As the editor, Dede Allen, described it, "We were able to go in with angles and close-ups and only pull back when we wanted to show what Arthur called 'the tapestry' [i.e., the social context of the period]. Arthur [Penn] really wanted to give it all this energy. He kept saying, 'Look at the film again. Make it go faster.' "[16]

We can see Penn and Allen making the film go faster more subtly through editing between scenes and within them. That cut from Bonnie's emerging question in the fields to Clyde's answer in the roadhouse is one example. She does not even articulate her question ["How do you know so much about me?"] before he answers it right after the edit, but there are many, many others. When we first meet C. W. Moss at the gas station, virtually every time we cut to him, he is already in motion, reacting to what Bonnie and Clyde have told him.

FIGURE 23
The composition of the last shot draws together various visual motifs.

Across the film, several scenes begin in close-up – though never with that extreme scale of Bonnie's first shot in the first scene – and establish the space only gradually, if at all. The questioning of the butcher in the hospital begins with a close-up of a mug shot and then one of the butcher's face before a quick medium shot orients us in space and time; one scene in the Joplin apartment begins on a close-up of the checkers game before the camera dollies back to pick up Bonnie pacing impatiently.

And the film is full of discontinuous cuts that its quick rhythms obscure – Clyde's matchstick is racing up and down in his mouth as he shows Bonnie his gun, or it is motionless in the reverse angle. As they run to the car after the first robbery, Bonnie asks Clyde his name. The first medium long shot shows her pulling back her hair with her left hand; in the second, closer shot, it is her right hand doing the impromptu coiffure (Figs. 24 and 25). At C. W.'s gas station, Bonnie is alternately slumped on her elbow or sitting upright. The scene with the farmer Otis Harris and his fieldhand has many roughly matched shots and cuts around the group in 360-degree space. None of these are as noticeable as the jump cut/burst wipe from Ivan Moss exiting the ice cream parlor to Frank Hamer in the same position, or the opening cuts of Bonnie in her room, or of course, the final ambush. Such incongruities bespeak a cavalier attitude toward continuity that produces a jolting, liberating film style.

Most dramatically, editing creates the breathless pace of the film, and this is established even in the film's credit sequence. A series of Walker Evans/Dorothea Lange–type, sepia photographs flash on the screen establishing the milieu of early 1930s rural America. We progress from family portraits to group shots: children and adults posed in front of a variety of settings – homes, schools, with their cars, with their horses, and in generic landscapes. Toward the end of the credit sequence, as the recording of Rudy Vallee singing "Deep Night" is in full swing, we look at men with guns in a variety of postures – holding the guns casually, aiming them, and so on.[17] The sequence concludes with single slides and titles introducing Clyde and Bonnie. Taken as a whole, this sequence traces the intertwining of family, friends, and romantic attachments in shaping the quality of individual lives in the rural South, much as the film will reveal family, friends, and romance – by their absence as much as by their presence – as the key elements in the career of of Bonnie and Clyde. Since the sequence progresses to shots of men casually bearing rifles and guns, it – along with the fading to red of the title letters[18] – previews Bonnie and Clyde's casual choice of violent action.

Because these are photographs, without motion, we can also attend to how they are juxtaposed. Sound effects suggest a camera shutter clicking; but as we begin to scan and comprehend each image, we are aware that whoever controls the camera is in a hurry. Most of the images flash by extremely quickly. Several are on screen for less than a second, and their ephemerality is highlighted by the longer film credits interspersed among them.

FIGURES 24 and 25
Ignoring details of continuity: Bonnie brushes her hair back with her left hand in the long shot, but uses her right hand in the cut-in.

It is impossible to engage with the specifics of any one photograph. The meaning of the images resides in their generic evocation of rural life and of extreme poverty, and before we have had time to barely recognize the subject of one photo, the next photo is upon us.

From its very first moments, then, *Bonnie and Clyde* uses editing to frustrate its audience's desire to know and dwell on the subjects it shows; what we see and will see are presented in a way that eludes a satisfying, rationalizing understanding, much in the way that the opening scene unfolds so quickly before us that we meet Clyde before we understand Bonnie, and they are both off and running when we have scarcely gotten to know them. The general milieu evoked by the photos could give us insight into Bonnie's behavior if we had the time to think about it, but we do not. "From tne beginning," John Cawelti has written, "the film establishes a restless, breathless pace."[19] My point here is that that pacing begins with the credits. Now we can appreciate that the opening scene with Bonnie actually sustains the confusion of the credit sequence and adds to it the jarring cutting.[20]

Yet, once Clyde is shown outside near Bonnie's mother's car in a cutaway shot (shot 5), the scene unfolds without the extreme close-ups and discontinuous cuts that introduced us to Bonnie, and progresses in a more conventional fashion, with crosscutting between Bonnie inside and at her window and Clyde below.[21] Fragmentation of space becomes the keynote of subsequent shots – only four shots in the first thirty (before the couple begin their walk into town) actually show them together in the same space. This kind of piecemeal construction will inform many of the film's later scenes, such as Clyde's first display of his gun, which is shot with all its phallic implications, even when Bonnie's hand touches it, in complete isolation from their bodies.[22]

What prevents Penn's approach here from veering into a French New Wave–style exploration of editing for editing's sake is that, for the rest of the film, Penn (like many directors trained in the theater) choreographs the actors' gestures, the camerawork, and the editing to amplify the action from the mise-en-scène up.[23] Consider Bonnie and Clyde's verbal sparring as they walk into town. During their stroll past drab houses, laundry lines, and empty yards, the camera slowly dollies alongside in a sixty-eight-second long take. Clyde playfully guesses at Bonnie's occupation (a movie star among them). The camera stops with Bonnie after Clyde suggests she is a maid; the insulted Bonnie asks, "What do you think I am?" and Clyde replies correctly, "You're a waitress." The camera resumes its movement as Bonnie regains her composure to ask Clyde what he does for a living when he is not stealing cars; the camera again stops when he reveals his jail term; it again moves with Bonnie when she recovers from this news, and it stops again when he mentions armed robbery. The alternating motion and stillness registers the shifting upper hand in their duel, as well as being allied with Bonnie's response. Sassy Bonnie gets the final word in the shot sequence, commenting, "The things that turn up in the street these days," as the camera pans left with her, leaving Clyde behind. The long take shot ends as Bonnie disappears behind a tree.

Their dalliance continues on a deserted Main Street in West Dallas. Now Penn and Allen substitute cutting for camerawork to visualize the seesaw dynamic of the couple's flirtatious taunts, particularly as they take turns breaking out of the camera frame. Clyde's mention of his amputated toes brings their stroll to a halt, and Bonnie's surprised reaction engenders a cut into medium close-up of them both. In his eagerness to show her the results of his surgery, Clyde pushes forward out of frame to a fire hydrant, leaving Bonnie behind – a movement picked up subsequently in long shot. In reply, Bonnie's refusal to look at his "dirty feet on Main Street" allows her to exit a subsequent medium shot and to leave Clyde behind. But Clyde gets the last word this time: in response to her asking him whether he *really* cut his toes off, he smiles without answering and clears frame to the right, before Bonnie follows him, leaving the frame empty, except for a view of the sky.[24]

The robbery and flight that result from the cramped scene of soda drinking and Bonnie's questioning of Clyde about armed robbery finally opens up the mise-en-scène with a sense of expanse and energy that, along with the Flatt and Scruggs "Foggy Mountain Breakdown" music, conveys the couple's exhilaration. The play of contention between Clyde and Bonnie that is visualized through abrupt movement within and out of the frame continues through the couple's argument in the fields after the first robbery, though it becomes less turbulent with each subsequent dispute.

In short, these early scenes evince an approach to camerawork and editing that conveys the ebb and flow of a conversation between two lively, imposturing malcontents and the uncertainty of their destination. Clearly, across these scenes, Bonnie has grown from intuitively curious about to absolutely fascinated with Clyde. The most convincing explanation of Penn's stylistic choices is that they visualize character subjectivity. John Cawelti, in keeping with his interpretive emphasis on Bonnie's sensibility, writes of the first long take in the film that "the tracking movement represents Bonnie's emotions at this point," and, "The halting of the camera movement at these points suggests the inner workings of Bonnie's mind. These are moments when she is confronted with something requiring deeper reflection and decision."[25] Cawelti later argues, of the extreme long shot of West Dallas as Clyde enters the grocery store: "The scene is filmed in such a way as to minimize our sense of the moral implications of Clyde's actions, as if to make us share Clyde's inability to recognize the suffering and pain that his actions cause."[26] We might alternately interpret the long shot as authorial commentary, a reminder of the drab milieu that the couple rebels against.

Our introduction to C. W. Moss replays the first encounter of

Bonnie and Clyde – another instance of the film's architectural resonance. The opening shot of that scene has framed C. W. claustrophobically in a medium long shot working on the car. Clyde is in the foreground right, rolling a cigarette, and Bonnie is in the mid-ground center, as they gesture to each other about C. W. and wait impatiently for the repair job to be finished. Thanks to Clyde's tutelage we can read C. W.'s circumstances: he is, like Bonnie, trapped in a boring job, to the point that he repeats her opening-sequence gesture by banging, hard and repeatedly, on a post when he learns who the couple is. Like Clyde, C. W. is accused of harassing little old ladies, and like Clyde, he must prove he has "guts" by walking into the store and taking out the cash. Clyde passed his test inside the West Dallas grocery store, where we could not see him; C. W., however, must complete his in our full view, through the gas station window. But this visibility of Moss's first robbery with Bonnie and Clyde is emblematic of the entire scene – whereas the opening sequence of the film is heavily fragmented into close-ups and cutaways, in the first scene with Moss we are from the very first shot oriented toward all the spatial relationships. In sum, the stylistic variety and organic unity of *Bonnie and Clyde* extends to its most minute details.

This extended analysis of *Bonnie and Clyde* demonstrates the film's eclectic stylistic arsenal, which is part of its strategy to convey to the audience the paradoxical qualities of its characters and its subject. We can attribute this strategy in part to *Bonnie and Clyde*'s being a film designed to make its audience profoundly uncomfortable. This strategy takes effect in the film's opening credits and in its very first opening scene; it continues through the film's differently paced shots and scenes and discontinuous cuts to its apocalyptic final moments.

Starting with *Bonnie and Clyde*'s premiere, much critical commentary on the film's distinctive look and feel focused on the film's affinities with European filmmaking. Carolyn Geduld described American critics in 1967 who interpreted the film as "a Hollywood response to the French 'take over' of American genres."[27] Robin Wood, in his 1969 monograph, suggested that "The New Wave's example of spontaneous inventiveness seems to have acted as a releasing rather than determining influence [on Penn]."[28]

Thirty years after the premiere, academic film critics concur. The most forceful exponent of this argument, Robert Ray, asserts that "The most important of the New American movies, *Bonnie and Clyde*, resembled a pastiche of New Wave effects," having taken its shifts in tone from *Shoot the Piano Player* and its fragmentary opening sequence of a hero in the midst of stealing a car from *Breathless*, which was the primary model for the film.[29] The "playfulness," "speed," and "lyricism" of Jean-Luc Godard and Francois Truffaut's earliest films bespoke their creators' obsession with film aesthetics: using long takes, jump cuts, slow motion, location shooting, and freeze frames, these filmmakers demonstrated the usefulness of such techniques to open-minded American directors.[30] But Ray argues that, in general, "new American cinema" directors "adopted only the New Wave's superficial stylistic exuberance, leaving Classic Hollywood's paradigms fundamentally untouched."[31] In *Bonnie and Clyde*, he contends, we can see the experimental potential of the French New Wave style being restricted to particular moments; formal conservatism informed the bulk of the film, "surrounding the borrowed New Wave devices with long stretches that completely conformed to traditional continuity rules."[32] In his extended study of Arthur Penn, Robert Kolker makes a similar point.[33]

These pronouncements ring with an almost moral disapproval, a disappointment that *Bonnie and Clyde* did not more fully embrace New Wave technique. Yet such judgments are arbitrary; the sheer artistry of *Bonnie and Clyde* absolutely justifies its status as a powerful landmark in Hollywood history. This is why subsequent couple-on-the-run films that depict amoral naïfs at odds with society (Terence Malick's *Badlands* [1972], Robert Altman's *Thieves Like Us* [1973], and Oliver Stone's *Natural Born Killers* [1994]), consistently refer back to *Bonnie and Clyde*.

When Penn's film is compared with Godard's work (as in Ray's argument), it seems conventional. But so does virtually every other narrative fiction film. One could also argue that the bulk of Truffaut's own films never repeated the exploratory playfulness of *Jules and Jim* or *Shoot the Piano Player*. By contrast, when Penn's film is compared with the bulk of Hollywood filmmaking of the last thirty years, *Bonnie and Clyde* remains a high point in Hollywood's attempts to extend the lexicon of visual style, to experiment with narrative structure, and most impressively of all, to complicate the relationship of cinematic heroes to the film viewer. Considering *Bonnie and Clyde*'s character construction, shifts in point of view, and visual style helps us appreciate the film's achievements.

NOTES

1. Robin Wood writes, "Penn brings us physically so close to his [characters] that it is difficult to remain detached" (*Arthur Penn* [New York: Praeger, 1969], 76). Wood's chapter on the film strikes me as still the most nuanced account of the character relationships within the film. Robert Kolker makes a similar point: "In *Bonnie and Clyde* no time is lost and no space between viewer and characters is allowed" (*A Cinema of Loneliness: Penn, Kubrick, Scorsese, Spielberg, Altman*, 2d ed. [New York: Oxford University Press, 1988], 32). John Cawelti was the first critic to argue that the opening close-up plunges us into the immediacy of Bonnie's world; see his "The Artistic Power of *Bonnie and Clyde*," in *Focus on "Bonnie and Clyde,"* John Cawelti, ed. (Englewood Cliffs, NJ: Prentice-Hall, 1973), 57–9.

2. Cawelti, "Artistic Power," 49, 68; and William J. Free, "Aesthetic and Moral Value in *Bonnie and Clyde*," in Cawelti, ed., *Focus on "Bonnie and Clyde,"* 103.

3. Wood, *Arthur Penn*, 83–4; and Cawelti, "Artistic Power," 71. On Bonnie's entrapment, see also Cawelti, "Artistic Power," 49, 68, and Free, "Aesthetic and Moral Value," 103; on the window motif of

the film, see Carolyn Geduld, *"Bonnie and Clyde:* Society vs. the Clan," in Cawelti, ed., *Focus on "Bonnie and Clyde,"* 96.

4. Kolker, *Cinema of Loneliness*, 32.
5. See Ibid., 26, for a description of a similar device in Penn's *Mickey One* (1964), where an extremely elaborate and bewildering credit sequence of "surreal" images is explained by a later dialogue scene. See my "Hollywood's Arty Cinema: John Ford's *The Long Voyage Home* (1940)," *Wide Angle* 10, no. 1 (1988): 30–1, for a discussion of a comparable approach to exposition in a Hollywood film nearly three decades earlier.
6. Cawelti, "Artistic Power," 61, refers to "sudden and impulsive cuts" in these scenes; Kolker, *Cinema of Loneliness* 32, writes of this scene, "The cutting is swift and arrhythmical; many of the shots are terminated before the physical action contained within them is finished."
7. Telephone interview with Arthur Penn, September 25, 1997.
8. On the escalation of violence through the film see Wood, *Arthur Penn*, 83–4, and Cawelti, "Artistic Power," 71.
9. Cawelti, "Artistic Power," 45, 48.
10. Wood, *Arthur Penn*, 85–6.
11. Ibid., 82.
12. About this, I disagree with Robert Ray's discussion of the film. Ray writes, "Clearly, Penn intended for his movie to work along Godardian (or Hitchcockian) principles: initial identification with the heroes, gradual withdrawal of sympathy, and final recognition of their errors and one's own complicity in them" (322). But *Bonnie and Clyde* does not work this way. There is no gradual withdrawal of sympathy for the heroes; or if there is (cued perhaps by the few scenes, late in the film, with Sheriff Hamer), it dissolves by the film's conclusion. Even given their actions throughout the film, Bonnie and Clyde are much more sympathetic after the attack that kills Buck and wounds them, and they are at their most sympathetic just before their deaths. See Robert Ray, *A Certain Tendency of the Hollywood Cinema, 1930–1950* (Princeton: Princeton University Press, 1985).
13. Cawelti, "Artistic Power," 50.
14. Ibid., 52.
15. Ibid., 68.
16. Ric Gentry, "An Interview with Dede Allen," *Film Quarterly* 46, no. 1 (Fall 1992): 21.
17. The music of the film has an equally contrapuntal quality, relative

to its images. Whereas the use of Vallee's "Deep Night" during the credits is conventional as a period piece, the song's juxtaposition with the photographs of the rural, depressed South give it a double-edged meaning: as Robin Wood writes, "It implies at once the need to transcend or escape from commonplace reality and the lack of any spiritual or intellectual training for finding a *valid* alternative." See Wood, *Arthur Penn*, 82.

18. Kolker, *Cinema of Loneliness*, 31.
19. Cawelti, "Artistic Power," 52.
20. About those photographs of Clyde and Bonnie – Clyde's appears likely to have been taken during the Parker family reunion; his clothes and cap are identical – an instance when the film cues the audience to some retrospective understanding of what it has seen. Is Bonnie's snapshot also taken from the picnic? It would seem to be, since she is not wearing her usually stylish gangster getup.
21. Kolker, *Cinema of Loneliness*, 32–4, stresses the centrality of shot–reverse shot as a fundamental device of Hollywood style that Penn uses reflectively throughout the film.
22. Previous critics have overlooked the first shot of Clyde and Bonnie together, arguing that establishing shots do not appear either until Bonnie comes downstairs (Cawelti, "Artistic Power," 63) or until Clyde enters the grocery store in West Dallas (Kolker, *Cinema of Loneliness*, 34); the latter action occurs seven minutes into the film, although Kolker claims it is fifteen.
23. See Penn's expressed admiration for Elia Kazan as the greatest director of actors, in Jim Hillier, "Arthur Penn," in Cawalt's ed., *Focus on "Bonnie and Clyde,"* 8.
24. It is worth briefly comparing this moment in the film with the films of Michelangelo Antonioni, such as *L'Avventura* (1959) or *L'Eclisse* (1962), which are full of empty shots that last several seconds as they begin and end; such shots compel the viewer to wonder why we are looking at the scene and when the characters will arrive. In *Bonnie and Clyde*, the absence of characters lasts only seconds, however.
25. Cawelti, "Artistic Power," 63 and 64.
26. Ibid., 68–9.
27. Geduld, *"Bonnie and Clyde,"* 93.
28. Wood, *Arthur Penn*, 72.
29. Ray, *A Certain Tendency*, 289.
30. In Ray's argument, the French New Wave techniques were made usable for Hollywood directors through the mediation of Richard

Lester's *A Hard Day's Night* (1963). See Ray, *A Certain Tendency*, 270–1.

31. Ray, *A Certain Tendency*, 287.
32. Ibid., 294.
33. Kolker, *Cinema of Loneliness*, 29.

STEPHEN PRINCE

The Hemorrhaging of American Cinema:

BONNIE AND CLYDE'S LEGACY OF CINEMATIC VIOLENCE

Bonnie and Clyde (1967) is a landmark film for many reasons, chief among them the film's presentation of graphic violence with a detail unprecedented in American cinema. When the the Texas Rangers ambush Bonnie and Clyde, the bloody, slow-motion deaths of the two outlaws have a ferocity that no American director before Arthur Penn dared attempt. The film's violence elicited outrage and controversy in its day, yet television now routinely presents the film without editing to tone down its visual intensity. The public response may have mellowed over time, but *Bonnie and Clyde* established a new threshold for screen violence. Subsequent filmmakers have felt compelled to surpass this threshold, so that today the violence in Penn's film seems tame compared to the carnage found in *Taxi Driver* (1976), *Casino* (1995), *Robocop* (1987), *Judge Dredd* (1995), and countless slice-and-dice horror films. Contemporary moviegoers display a voracious appetite for screen violence, and filmmakers eagerly serve up dripping corpses in pursuit of box office dollars.

Because one of the roots of the graphic violence so plentiful in modern cinema can be traced back to *Bonnie and Clyde*, it is

127

instructive to examine Penn's film in relation to both the cultural conditions that made it possible and the ultraviolent legacy it bequeathed to modern cinema. I will first examine *Bonnie and Clyde* against the social events of the era, spotlighting the changing regulations on movie content that opened the door to graphic violence. Next, I will look closely at the visual structure of the final ambush in order to understand the techniques that Penn used to intensify the impact of the deaths of Bonnie and Clyde. Finally, I will survey screen violence after *Bonnie and Clyde*, with an emphasis on the debates about the social effects of movie violence that *Bonnie and Clyde* helped fuel in the late sixties.

Time magazine devoted its December 8, 1967 cover story to the new wave of unconventional American films that began to appear late in the 1960s. These pictures included not only *Bonnie and Clyde* but also *In the Heat of the Night* (1967), *The Graduate* (1967), and *Reflections in a Golden Eye* (1967). The article pointed out that these films and others "are now treating once-shocking themes with a maturity and candor unthinkable even five years ago" (p. 67). Focusing on *Bonnie and Clyde*, the article hailed the film as "a watershed picture," pointing out that its violence "was a commentary on the mindless daily violence of the American '60s" (p. 67). The extraordinary social unrest of the period was a major influence upon Penn's visualization of the carnage that concludes the picture. It was no coincidence that American films became bloodier than ever at the same time as the nation was waging an unpopular war in Southeast Asia and confronting a domestic scene marked by urban riots, campus protests against the war, and recurrent political assassinations. By the end of 1967, the Vietnam War was at its height. American troop levels had reached four hundred sixty thousand (thirteen thousand had already died), and mass protests against the war were drawing crowds of one hundred thousand at demonstrations in New York and Washington, D.C. Riots during the first nine months of 1967 erupted in 127 cities. Nearly fourteen thousand people were arrested in just 22 of these cities (National Advisory Commission on Civil Disorders, 1968).

The National Commission on the Causes and Prevention of Violence reported that from 1963 to 1968 more than two million persons participated in social protest. "Civil rights demonstrations mobilized 1.1 million, anti-war demonstrations 680,000, and ghetto riots an estimated 200,000. Nine thousand casualties resulted, including some 200 deaths" (National Commission on the Causes and Prevention of Violence, p. 51). Coincident with such episodes of mass protest, the national rates of violent crimes rose significantly during the decade. Steep increases in homicide, rape, aggravated assault, and robbery fed a sharp public fear of street crime and a perception that a wave of violence was sweeping over American society (National Commission on the Causes and Prevention of Violence, p. 16). The high-profile assassinations of Robert F. Kennedy and Martin Luther King in 1968 traumatized the nation and led historian Arthur Schlesinger, Jr., speaking as Kennedy lay dying, to decry the American "compulsion toward violence" (Schlesinger, p. 20).

The Vietnam War and the disintegration of civil society that accompanied it helped put the subject of violence on the national agenda in an urgent and ominous way. Writing about young student radicals, sociologist Kenneth Keniston famously noted that "the issue of violence is to this generation what the issue of sex was to the Victorian world" (Keniston, p. 248). Sociologist Todd Gitlin, a former member of the Students for a Democratic Society (SDS), diagnosed the violence as "the siren song of the late sixties" (Gitlin, p. 6), noting that the violence had become a topic in the fantasy life of the entire society. The sociopolitical turmoil of these years left an indelible mark on American culture. Its impact on cinema helped produce what *Time* labeled "the shock of the new" in describing a new generation of films whose style and content represented a decisive break with the past.

Within this context, *Bonnie and Clyde*'s director, Arthur Penn, and his collaborators conceived of Bonnie and Clyde as representative figures for the time. Rejecting the studio's suggestion that they film the movie in black and white and aim for historical accuracy, Penn and Warren Beatty, the producer, agreed that the film, metaphorically and by implication, had to deal with the 1960s in its portrait of young Depression-era rebels who resist the Establishment. Penn later said he thought the film was successful in these terms because it "caught the spirit of the times and the true radical nature of the kids . . . because here were these two who, instead of knuckling under to the system, resisted it" (Crowdus and Porton, p. 9). He added that the outlaw couple were intended to be "paradigmatic figures for our times" (Crowdus and Porton, p. 9). About the film's violence, Penn expressed his belief that its graphic images were far less bloody than the television news imagery of the Vietnam War that Americans were watching daily in their living rooms: "it didn't even occur to me, particularly, that it was a violent film. Not given the times in which we were living, because every night on the news we saw kids in Vietnam being airlifted out in body bags, with blood all over the place" (Crowdus and Porton, p. 9). As these remarks indicate, Penn considered the film's make-believe violence appropriate and justifiable within its real-world context of America fighting an unpopular and bloody war and engulfed by domestic strife.

Although Penn's justification begs the issue of the effects of graphic movie violence on the society that consumes it, his remarks demonstrate the salience of the era's sociopolitical violence for his artistic orientation and his design of the film. (And its salience for his other films, as well. Penn includes references to the assassinations of John F. and Robert Kennedy in *The Chase* [1963] and *Night Moves* [1975]. In *Bonnie and Clyde*, when Clyde is shot, a piece of his head flies off in acknowledgment of President Kennedy's killing as captured in the 8mm documentary footage shot by Abraham Zapruder.) The Vietnam War and domestic social unrest directly shaped the film's social symbolism

FIGURE 26
Bonnie and Clyde: violence as the "siren song" of the late 1960s.

and, more generally, contributed to a cultural climate focused on the anxieties and traumas caused by violence. This climate was a precondition for Penn's ability to visualize graphic violence in ways he believed were nonexploitative and socially significant.

Such a climate was, however, insufficient for the making of *Bonnie and Clyde*. A combination of social, artistic, and institutional factors made this film possible. On the institutional side, changes in regulations governing movie content offered filmmakers in the late 1960s more creative freedom than they could have had earlier and actually provided them with incentives to transgress social mores. Two crucial changes in particular gave filmmakers the freedom they needed to make pictures like *Bonnie and Clyde*: (1) the revision in September 1966 of Hollywood's thirty-six-year-old Production Code and (2) the creation two years later of the Code and Rating Administration (CARA) with its G-M-R-X film classification system.

The old Production Code had imposed a lengthy list of rules on filmmakers that stipulated how such subjects as love, marriage, crime, religion, and sexuality had to be portrayed on screen. Concerning crime, films were specifically forbidden to give close visual attention to weapons, to shootings, or to brutal deaths in just the ways that *Bonnie and Clyde* did. The 1966 revision of the Production Code by the Motion Picture Association of America (MPAA) effectively scrapped the old code's extensive content rules and substituted ten broad guiding principles (e.g., "Restraint shall be exercised in portraying the taking of life"). The revised code was designed to move cinema closer to the mores characteristic of modern society and a more permissive era and to expand the creative freedom of filmmakers (Chapin, p. 5). The MPAA, which is made up of major film companies, promoted its revised code over the objections of theater owners and social watchdog groups concerned about the rising amount of profanity, violence, and sex in new films. Viewers who complained about profanity or violence in films were told by the MPAA that they "fail to realize that films have changed to reflect our changing culture" (*Variety*, Mar. 6, 1969, p. 7).

By placing film in the vanguard of social change, the MPAA helped spearhead and defend filmmakers' creative freedom. MPAA president Jack Valenti praised the "new breed" of non-conformist director, whose emergence, he believed, typified the most important artistic trend in then-contemporary American film. Testifying on December 19, 1968 before the National Commission on the Causes and Prevention of Violence (convened in part because of the new graphic movie violence), Valenti defended *Bonnie and Clyde* against the committee's criticism that the film was too violent. He proudly announced, "There is a new breed of filmmaker. And mark you well this new filmmaker, because he's an extraordinary fellow. He's young. He's sensitive. He's dedicated. He's reaching out for new dimensions of expression. And he's not bound – not bound – by the conventions of a conformist past. I happen to think that's good" (*Mass Media Hearings*, p. 193).

Valenti's defense of American cinema's creative direction was reflected in the production policies of the young top executives at Warner Brothers–Seven Arts (which produced *Bonnie and Clyde*), Twentieth Century–Fox, and Paramount studios. These executives supported new styles of pictures and granted directors greater creative latitude in their productions. Penn used this new climate to make a film that audaciously mixed slapstick humor with graphic violence. He could do so because the industry recognized that the youth market was sizable (by 1968, 48% of box office admissions were from the 16–24 age group) ("Pix Must Broaden Market," *Variety*, Mar. 20, 1968, p. 1), that unconventional films appealed to this market, and crucially, that screen violence could be hugely profitable.

By 1967 the trend toward harder-edged and more graphic movie violence was unmistakable. The violence in three European Westerns distributed by United Artists in the United States – *A Fistful of Dollars*, *A Few Dollars More*, and *The Good, the Bad, and the Ugly* – was far more cold-blooded and plentiful than that in the Hollywood product. These films did phenomenal business, which critics linked to their violent content (Landry, p. 7). In July and August 1967 came the premieres of Robert Aldrich's *The Dirty Dozen*, a cynical and savage World War II film, and Penn's *Bonnie and Clyde*; together, they ignited a storm of controversy over movie violence. Bosley Crowther devoted several of his columns in the *New York Times* to trashing these two films, warning, "By habituating the public to violence and brutality . . . films of excessive violence only deaden their sensitivities and make slaughter seem a meaningless cliché" (Crowther, p. 10). In the first of two pieces on *Bonnie and Clyde*, Joseph Morgenstern, *Newsweek*'s reviewer, condemned the film for possessing "some of the most gruesome carnage since Verdun" (Morgenstern, Aug. 21, 1967, p. 65); he reversed himself on the film's merit the following week, although he still maintained that the picture's "gore goes too far" and that *The Dirty Dozen* was a "trash" film awash in "a river of blood" (Morgenstern, Aug. 2, 1967, p. 82).

But blood was profitable. *The Dirty Dozen* became the top-grossing film of 1967, and although *Bonnie and Clyde* earned only $2.5 million in 1967, by July 1968, it had earned $28 million on its $2.5 million production cost (*Variety*, Aug. 7, 1968, p. 1). So extraordinary was the repeat business for *Bonnie and Clyde* that *Variety* placed it in an "impossible to project" category (*Variety*, Aug. 7, 1968, p. 1). The film landed twenty-two times on *Variety*'s weekly list of the top dozen box office earners, at the time a record surpassed only by *Mary Poppins* (thirty-two times in late 1964–early 1965) ("Persevering of 'Bonnie and Clyde,' " *Variety*, Mar. 20, 1968, p. 5). The box office performance of *Bonnie and Clyde* would encourage other filmmakers, such as Sam Peckinpah, to make their own explorations of ultraviolence. *Bonnie and Clyde*'s stunning popularity validated the decision of Valenti, the MPAA, and top studio executives to bring movies into line with changing social mores and with the more permissive American culture emerging from these changes.

Had *Bonnie and Clyde* been a routine or mediocre piece of filmmaking, however, its popularity probably would not have been as great as it was, and certainly its place in film history would be very diminished. But *Bonnie and Clyde* was cutting-edge filmmaking, in tune with profound shifts in American culture and employing the forms and techniques of cinema style in daringly new ways. Of all the film's stylistic innovations, Penn's visualization of Bonnie and Clyde's deaths has had the most lasting impact on American cinema. Subsequent filmmakers might take slow-motion ballets of blood to much greater extremes, but Penn was the first American filmmaker to conjoin multicamera filming, montage editing, and slow motion systematically in the visualization of screen violence. Penn and his crew joined four cameras side by side, each running at a different speed, to film the death scene. The differing speeds enabled Penn, in the editing, to shift among different rates of slow motion (produced by operating the camera at a higher-than-normal rate of speed) and to intercut them with shots of the action taken at normal speed. In the last scene, Penn used montage editing (the cutting together of very brief shots to form a sequence or scene) to capture an enormous amount of detail and to convey this detail at a furious pace. From the point at which the flock of birds abruptly flies off, signaling the start of the ambush, to the final image in *Bonnie and Clyde*, after the shooting has ceased, the sequence contains fifty-one shots and runs for fifty-four seconds.

The quickest cutting occurs just before the posse opens fire, as Bonnie and Clyde, aware of what is about to happen, glance at each other in a rush of panic. In four seconds, nine images flash by on-screen. Penn and his editor, Dede Allen, dynamically intercut slow motion with normal speed and employ differing rates of slow motion in this scene. In the sequence, time becomes quite elastic because the internal rhythms of the shots vary considerably, depending on the speed at which they occur. By alternating the tempo between slow and apparently accelerated (the apparent acceleration was produced at normal speed

FIGURES 27, 28, and 29
By using multiple cameras operating at different speeds, Penn visualized violent death with unprecedented vividness.

by the rate of automatic fire), Penn vividly brings out the alternately balletic and spastic qualities of the scene (Crowdus and Porton, p. 9).

Furthermore, by intercutting slow- and normal-speed action, Penn creates a more kinetic and intense scene. The way the action accelerates and decelerates keeps the viewer perceptually off balance. By intercutting the slow-motion with normal-tempo footage, Penn sustains the dynamic tension between the film speeds, overcoming the tendency of slow motion to cause the action to bog down and to convey inertia. If slow motion lasts too long on-screen, the action slogs along and loses its physicality because the actors seem unaffected by gravity. But keeping the slow-motion inserts brief surmounts these inertial tendencies, and, when intercut with normal-speed action, the slow-motion inserts become dynamic. This energy is not in the slow motion itself. (As just noted, slow motion tends to de-energize the action.) It is contained in the referencing of slow-motion with normal-speed action. If the slow-motion inserts only briefly disrupt the normal-speed action, the contrasting tempo becomes quite dynamic, with the normal-speed action energizing the slow-motion insert. Penn did not immediately grasp this principle, as an earlier film in his career clearly demonstrates.

Penn previously used slow motion in *The Left-Handed Gun* (1958) in a scene in which Billy the Kid shoots Bob Ollinger, one of Pat Garrett's deputies. As Billy shoots Ollinger, Penn cuts to a slow-motion shot of Ollinger flailing his arms, then to a fast-motion shot of Ollinger hitting the ground. The contrast between the slow and fast motion is too extreme and jarring to work effectively in this film (as we have seen, brief slow-motion inserts contrast quite effectively with normal-speed action). Moreover, the slow motion is not judiciously matched with an appropriate screen action. Ollinger's arm flailing is neither balletic nor spastic in the ways that the convulsions of Bonnie and Clyde are, and by using only one slow-motion insert in a scene that does not feature montage editing, Penn neither makes time elastic nor creates explosive rhythms, as he does in the later film's montage.

Penn acknowledged that he was just experimenting with the medium when he made *The Left-Handed Gun* (Crowdus and Porton, p. 5), whereas his conclusion for *Bonnie and Clyde* incorporated a sophisticated and systematically conceived design. It is important, however, to stress the limits of Penn's originality with respect to this design. Although Penn was the first American director to demonstrate potency for visualizing screen violence, and thus become a mentor for directors of violence who came later, such as Sam Peckinpah, Penn was not the discoverer or inventor of these techniques. Instead, he borrowed them from the films of the Japanese director Akira Kurosawa and was gracious enough to admit this. In discussing his conception for the final scene, Penn said that stylistically he wanted to launch the outlaw couple into legend by making the violence of their death look balletic: "having seen enough Kurosawa by that point, I knew how to do it" (Crowdus and Porton, p. 9).

Kurosawa began utilizing slow motion to convey violent action as early as his first film, *Sanshiro Sugata* (1943), but his best-known work in this connection is *The Seven Samurai* (1954), which Penn specifically cites as an inspiration (see Penn's essay in this volume). In a way that was very instructive for Penn, Kurosawa cuts in and out of the slow motion in *The Seven Samurai* to achieve maximum contrast and impact from the slow- and normal-speed footage. During the scene in which the leader of the samurai, Kambei (Takashi Shimura), rescues a kidnapped child from a crazed thief, Kurosawa strikingly intercuts footage filmed at normal speed with slow-motion footage, so that the rhythm of the scene fluctuates between these two different modes of time. The mortally wounded thief crashes through the hut's doorway to the village square outside where his dying is witnessed by amazed onlookers. Kurosawa intercuts three shots of the thief in slow motion – crashing through the door, running a few steps forward, and rising up on tiptoe – with three shots of the onlookers' reactions at normal speed. Since movement also occurs in these normal-speed shots, an extended internal tension between the differing modes of time builds up within the scene. In addition, Kurosawa routinely employed multiple cameras for capturing action, sometimes as many as five cameras at a time. By enlarging the visual perspective on the action, the cameras gave the director more material to use in constructing his montages.

Penn applied the general design of Kurosawa's rendition of screen violence to the death scene in *Bonnie and Clyde* with such brilliance that he decisively overturned decades of polite, bloodless movie violence in the American cinema. Furthermore, he accomplished this during a period when the film's graphic violence could resonate with the violence of America's Southeast Asian war and urban turmoil. Also at this time, Hollywood was abandoning its decades of rigid, in-house censorship and extending a welcome to nonconformist directors and unconventional styles. Penn was fortunate in that his stylistic interests and artistic vision coincided with these particular sociocultural circumstances and institutional changes.

The violence that concludes *Bonnie and Clyde* is a seminal

moment in American cinema and one attributable to these particular preconditions. As noted earlier, Penn defended the film's violence by pointing out that contemporary real-world violence was far more terrible than anything he had shown on the screen. "Why, suddenly, the cinema had to be immaculate, I'll never know," he said (Crowdus and Porton, p. 9). The head of the MPAA, Jack Valenti, also argued that the violence in films paled next to that shown in televised images from the Vietnam War: "For the first time in the history of this country, people are exposed to instant coverage of a war in progress. When so many movie critics complain about violence on film, I don't think they realize the impact of thirty minutes on the Huntley-Brinkley newscast – and that's real violence" (*Variety*, Feb. 21, 1968, p. 2). Both Penn and Valenti suggested that under certain conditions graphic screen violence can be justified because movie violence is not real. In the late sixties, social critics like directors Penn and Peckinpah began using explicit gore in their films to comment on the social violence of the era, and thus a case can be made for the progressive or beneficial value of their movies' graphic violence. In the films of Penn and Peckinpah, the violence is generally an index of social oppression or corruption and, therefore, a form of social criticism.

In the three decades since *Bonnie and Clyde*'s premiere, however, the blood has flowed profusely in American cinema. Moviegoers now commonly view severed ears (*Reservoir Dogs*), dismembered limbs (*Total Recall*), bodies beaten to a bloody pulp (*Casino*), and numerous other types of bloodletting and physical abuse. Therefore, our current perspective on movie violence is necessarily different from that of the late sixties, when Valenti could stress the benefits of bringing "old movie standards out of the archaic and arcane and into current trends" (*Variety*, Feb. 21, 1968, p. 2). To understand the legacy of *Bonnie and Clyde* in terms of movie violence, we must consider the research that has been done on the social effects of viewing graphic violence and answer the question of whether today anything progressive or beneficial can result from explicit cinema gore.

In the late sixties *Bonnie and Clyde* helped ignite discussion about the social effects of viewing screen violence, just as the era's social and political turmoil contributed to the public debate over the causes and prevention of violence in American society. Among the topics explored by the National Commission on the Causes and Prevention of Violence, convened in 1968, was violence in the media. Several commission members expressly criticized *Bonnie and Clyde* as a film that glorified violence. One commissioner, who called the film "the personification of violence for profit" (*Mass Media Hearings*, p. 207), pointed to a murder in his congressional district that he alleged had been inspired by the film. But social scientist Leonard Berkowitz, testifying before the committee, speculated that the film's graphic gore probably inhibited violence that otherwise might be inspired by the movie because it showed how awful violence was (*Mass Media Hearings*, p. 43).

Since *Bonnie and Clyde*, much research has been done on whether viewing violence on-screen tends to inhibit or to induce aggression in people; the bulk of the evidence supports the position that media violence has aggression-inducing properties. The studies have shown that the specific content of a television show or film correlates with aggressive responses by its viewers. Whenever the aggressive behavior of a character in a story is rewarded, it tends to elicit more imitative aggression from the story's viewers. Albert Bandura, who has argued persuasively for a social-learning theory of aggression rather than the view that aggression is an essential drive or instinct, points out that the rewards reaped from successful villainy "may overwhelm the viewer's value systems," even if the villains are punished by story's end (Bandura, Ross, and Ross, 1963b, p. 605; see also Bandura, Ross, and Ross, 1963a). When a film or television program presents aggression as a justifiable response to some prior event (e.g., Rocky's beating of the Soviet boxer to avenge Apollo Creed's death in *Rocky IV*), the depiction may have a disinhibiting effect on some viewers (see Berkowitz and Rawlings). When the aggression-evoking characteristics of film victims match the characteristics of available targets in everyday life, aggressive responses toward these real-life targets become more likely. The incineration of a Manhattan subway token clerk that followed the release of the film *Money Train*, which depicts a similar incident, would seem to exemplify this principle, but it has also been demonstrated experimentally (see Berkowitz and Geen).

In addition, film violence that is painless, that lacks evidence of a victim's suffering, tends to disinhibit some viewers (see Baron; Saunders and Baron). Viewers also may enjoy the film violence more when marked expressions of suffering by victims are omitted (see Blanchard, Graczyk, and Blanchard). Finally, heavy viewing of violent media content tends to desensitize viewers (see Cline, Croft, and Courrier). These individuals react to screen violence with less emotion and a lower physiological response than do occasional viewers. None of this empirical evidence is predictive of how a particular viewer will respond to screen violence. But it does demonstrate that a statistically significant number of viewers in a large population will find the specific content characteristics of screen violence to be an inducer or a disinhibitor of aggressive behavior.

In popular films – when Rocky patriotically pummels his robotic Soviet opponent in *Rocky IV*, or when Judge Dredd righteously guns down violent criminals, or when Bonnie and Clyde machine-gun the local police – these scenarios are presented as instances of justifiable aggression, and the victims politely cooperate by collapsing without a whimper. In his influential discussion of violence in the arts, John Fraser pointed to why audiences seem to enjoy the violence of *Bonnie and Clyde*: "since their [Bonnie and Clyde's] victims were a set of walking clichés whose death could disturb no one, even their violences were fun" (Fraser, p. 26). Fraser believed that the film is morally indifferent to the fates of the outlaw couple's victims. Penn himself seems to display an indifference to the consequences for the victims of Bonnie and Clyde's murder spree, when he remarked,

"Yes, they killed some people, but they got killed in the end, so they were heroic and martyred in that respect" (Crowdus and Porton, p. 9). Part of this indifference comes out of the traditions of the gangster film genre, which never cared much about the gangsters' bloody victims. But as I show in *Savage Cinema*, indifference has also now become a structural characteristic of modern screen violence.

In the graphic gore with which the film concludes, *Bonnie and Clyde* demonstrates the techniques by which screen violence can be turned into an exciting spectacle that is self-enclosed and detachable from the narrative. The technical components of Penn's scene – multicameras, montage editing, slow motion, and exploding bloodbags – have become the essential means for transforming movie violence into a visual spectacle that is both charged and appealing. Such spectacularized violence is often disconnected from the pain and suffering of its bloody victims. The death scene at the end of *Bonnie and Clyde* is remarkable because of the incredible firepower deployed against the outlaw couple and the close attention the film gives to the physical impact of the bullets; yet the scene lacks a sustained sense of the emotional and psychological components of Bonnie and Clyde's death agonies. The viewpoint of the scene is entirely exterior and physical. This is typical of such violent montages, which are almost always preoccupied with visualizing the mechanics of violent death (how a windshield explodes or a body convulses) rather than with the inner, emotional or psychological, consequences of violent trauma. The emotional costs of violence and its psychological impact on both victim and perpetrator are usually omitted from the stylistic and moral design of the montage-based approach to spectacularized death. But it is in these areas of impact that the human toll exacted by violence is demonstrated. Confined to visualizing the external, physical features of violent death, the montage aesthetic employed in cinema since *Bonnie and Clyde* rarely goes inside the eye of violence to render the psychological impact and emotional consequences.

The moral perspective that most scenes of spectacular violence offer their viewers is problematic. If filmmakers contend that their interest lies in dramatizing how awful violence is or if they express dismay at the vigilante responses such scenes arouse in audiences, their stance is contradicted by their evident pleasure in their craft, in the designing, shooting, and editing of these violent montage scenes. Penn describes his conception of *Bonnie and Clyde*'s ending as "a kind of epiphany," and Martin Scorsese remarks on the intense pleasure he derived from filming the bloody carnage at the end of *Taxi Driver* (DeCurtis, p. 211). Audiences excited by these scenes are simply sharing in the filmmakers' evident pleasure and responding to the filmmakers' manipulations. Penn unquestionably wanted the violence in *Bonnie and Clyde* to have a radical and metaphorical edge, to dramatize a rebellion against an intolerable social condition and to establish the martyrdom through violent death of the rebels. Thirty years later, however, after the legacy of spectacularized violence that *Bonnie and Clyde* helped establish, we should ask if graphic violence is any longer an element of style and narrative that has progressive or radical potential.

Viewers today have seen every manner of imaginable cinema death, and the research on the effects of viewing screen violence clearly demonstrates that such viewing teaches some viewers modes of aggression that they incorporate into their cognitive repertoire of possible behaviors. Creatively, little new can be done in visualizing violent death. Even the rare effort today to use graphic violence morally, to condemn that violence, can backfire. In one sobering example, the horrendous violence in *Schindler's List* (1994) was greeted with laughter by some Los Angeles schoolchildren who found the way in which the Nazis' victims fell to the ground after being shot in the head "kind of funny." Informed of their reaction, Steven Spielberg, the film's director, professed amazement at the desensitization of these viewers.

Today, screen violence has largely lost its power to shock, and ultraviolent films now require a benumbed response from their viewers. Director Quentin Tarantino counts on such a reaction when, in *Pulp Fiction*, he plays for comedy the scene in which a gunshot victim's head explodes in the backseat of a car, leaving a mess for the car's other occupants to clean. Todd Gitlin has noted the psychic price that viewers of modern ultraviolence pay for watching sadomasochistic screen spectacles: "The unprecedented violence wrought in Arthur Penn's 1967 *Bonnie and Clyde* punctured numbness; it did, as Pauline Kael wrote at the time, 'put the sting back in death.' But over the years of chain saws, sharks, abdomen-ripping aliens, and the like, movie violence has come to require, and train, numbness" (Gitlin, 1991, p. 247).

In this context, the epochal, radical bloodletting in *Bonnie and Clyde* has been overwhelmed and overtaken by the mechanized spectacles of violence it helped inaugurate. If now the violence in Penn's film seems tame and unremarkable, that is simply a register of what *Bonnie and Clyde* and subsequent films have done to the sensibilities of their viewers. In the late sixties, graphic cinema violence was the cutting edge of a revolution in screen style and content. Today, that edge has slashed into the moral sensibilities of viewers, as films cultivate their audiences' appetite for screen brutality and reinforce a generalized, diffuse cultural anxiety about a modern society that is perceived as very dangerous and violent (see Bogart Gerbner and Gross).

The bloody montage that concludes *Bonnie and Clyde* was both a beginning and an end. It inaugurated the modern cinema of ultraviolence, but this cinema has itself reached a creative and cultural dead end, even as box office cash registers continue to ring in movie theaters across the country. People grow more uneasy and more frightened about the world in which they live, and filmmakers remain fascinated with their abilities to mount flamboyant spectacles of gore and death. The radical gestures of Penn, Peckinpah, and other filmmakers of the late sixties have led to films of uninhibited sadomasochism, to epic visions of bloodshed and death. Instead of a radical, utopian social vision, the cinematic sadomasochism of today offers rage and nihilism. And there is no end in sight.

WORKS CITED

Bandura, Albert, Dorothea Ross, and Sheila A. Ross. "Imitation of Film-Mediated Aggressive Models." *Journal of Abnormal and Social Psychology* 66, no. 1 (1963): 3–11.

"Vicarious Reinforcement and Imitative Learning." *Journal of Abnormal and Social Psychology* 67, no. 6 (1963): 605.

Baron, Robert A. "Magnitude of Victim's Pain Cues and Level of Prior Arousal on Determinants of Adult Aggressive Behavior." *Journal of Personality and Social Psychology* 17, no. 3 (1971): 236–43.

Berkowitz, Leonard, and Russell G. Geen. "Film Violence and the Cue Properties of Available Targets." *Journal of Personality and Social Psychology* 3, no. 5 (1966): 525–30.

Berkowitz, Leonard, and Edna Rawlings. "Effects of Film Violence on Inhibitions against Subsequent Aggression." *Journal of Abnormal and Social Psychology* 66, no. 5 (1963): 405–12.

Blanchard, D. Caroline, Barry Graczyk, and Robert J. Blanchard. "Differential Reactions of Men and Women to Realism, Physical Damage, and Emotionality in Violent Films." *Aggressive Behavior* 12 (1986): 45–59.

Bogart, Leo. "Violence in the Mass Media." *Television Quarterly* 8, no. 3 (Summer 1969): 36–47.

" 'Brutal Films Pale Before Televised Vietnam' – Valenti." *Variety,* 21 February 1968.

Chapin, Louis. "New Movie Standards: General Film Code, Not Specific Bans." *Christian Science Monitor,* 23 September 1966.

Cline, Victor R., Roger G. Croft, and Steven Courrier. "Desensitization of Children to Television Violence." *Journal of Personality and Social Psychology* 27, no. 3 (1973): 360–5.

Crowdus, Gary, and Richard Porton. "The Importance of a Singular, Guiding Vision: An Interview with Arthur Penn." *Cineaste* 20, no. 2 (Spring 1993).

Crowther, Bosley. "A Smash at Violence." *New York Times,* 30 July 1967.

DeCurtis, Anthony. "What the Streets Mean: An Interview with Martin Scorsese." In *Plays, Movies, and Critics,* edited by Jody McAuliffe, p. 211. Durham, NC: Duke University Press, 1983.

Fraser, John. *Violence in the Arts*. New York: Cambridge University Press, 1976.

Gerbner, George, and Larry Gross. "Living With Television: The Violence Profile." *Journal of Communication* 26 (1976): 173–99.

Gitlin, Todd. "On Thrills and Kills: Sadomasochism in the Movies." *Dissent* (Spring 1991): 247.

———. *The Sixties: Years of Hope, Days of Rage*. New York: Bantam Books, 1989.

"Hollywood: The Shock of Freedom in Films." *Time*, 8 December 1967.

Keniston, Kenneth. *Young Radicals*. New York: Harvest, 1968.

Landry, Robert J. "It's Murder, Italian Style." *Variety*, 8 February 1967.

Mass Media Hearings. Vol. 9A: *A Report to the National Commission on the Causes and Prevention of Violence*. Washington, DC: U.S. Government Printing Office, 1969.

Morgenstern, Joseph. "The Thin Red Line." *Newsweek*, 28 August 1967.

———. "Two for a Tommy Gun." *Newsweek*, 21 August 1967.

National Advisory Commission on Civil Disorders. *Report*. Washington, DC: U.S. Government Printing Office, 1968.

National Commission on the Causes and Prevention of Violence. *To Establish Justice, to Ensure Domestic Tranquility: The Final Report of the National Commission on the Causes and Prevention of Violence*. New York: Praeger, 1970.

"Persevering of '*Bonnie and Clyde*.' " *Variety*, 20 March 1968.

"Pix Must Broaden Market." *Variety*, 20 March 1968.

Prince, Stephen. *Savage Cinema: Sam Peckinpah and the Rise of Ultraviolent Movies*. Austin: University of Texas Press, 1999.

Saunders, Glenn S., and Robert Steven Baron. "Pain Cues and Uncertainty as Determinants of Aggression in a Situation Involving Repeated Instigation." *Journal of Personality and Social Psychology* 32, no. 3 (1975): 495–502.

Schlesinger, Arthur, Jr. "American 1968: The Politics of Violence." *Harper's Magazine*, August 1968.

"Theatre Operators and Public Require Updating on Social Point of View." *Variety*, 6 March 1969.

"Warren Beatty 'Bonnie' Share." *Variety*, 7 August 1968.

Erasure and Taboo

A QUEER READING OF *BONNIE AND CLYDE*

I first saw *Bonnie and Clyde* in New York City in 1967 and loved its sense of freedom from authority. I was visiting my grandparents for a few days before beginning my second year at McGill University in Montreal. My date was a nice Jewish boy, a student I had met that summer in Israel, where we had attended an international choir festival. Later, our choir hosted his at Expo 67. Now, I was being escorted around this amazing city: Little Italy, Greenwich Village – the ethnic sights and sounds that make New York City so alive and inclusive. Going to see *Bonnie and Clyde* and returning to my grandparents' West Side rent-controlled apartment late at night, on the back of a motorcycle, squired by the most handsome and exciting man I had ever met, was as subversive as my life got in those days.

In 1995, I watched the film again. In the intervening years, *Bonnie and Clyde* had come to occupy an exalted place on almost every film critic's Ten Best Films list, so I was looking forward to the experience of reliving the mad chase, the frenetic music, and the stunning ending. But this was not all that I saw. I now saw *Bonnie and Clyde* as an evocative film about the fluidity of social constructions such as identity, family, and race. In short, I saw a powerfully queer movie.

148

I pondered this two-for-the-price-of-one quality of perception and asked myself several questions. Is my current gaze, as a lesbian, different? Am I seeing things queer because I have shifted my focus to frame my desire? Are movies queer only when they are made specifically by and for queers? When a queer reading is offered for an ostensibly heterosexual movie, such as my current reading of *Bonnie and Clyde*, is it a scholarly addition to the discussion or a politically inspired intrusion? My answer to myself, after careful consideration, re-viewing, and research, is not that my lesbianism has brought the homoerotic qualities of *Bonnie and Clyde* to the fore, but that the homophobic attitudes and machinations of the filmmakers failed to hide those qualities from my gaze.

Although we cannot read into a literary or cinematic text that which is not there, we can, by careful reading, tease out a fabric the author or filmmaker might have worked hard to mask to make the product marketable. So it is with the queer subtext of the movie *Bonnie and Clyde*: although the director and producer thought it best to hide the film's queer thread, it is in the movie nonetheless, and can be traced from the original (subversive) screenplay to the final (commercial) cut.[1] Because *Bonnie and Clyde* is widely considered a film about subversion – about outlaws who challenge a corrupt system and win our hearts before they die – it is important to challenge the film's deliberate suppression of sexual transgression. What I am suggesting is that by not daring enough, by denying the queer, Penn falls short of greatness, and his work remains, despite his aspirations, a well-crafted but disturbingly dishonest movie.

One weakness of *Bonnie and Clyde* is its presentation of a well-worn narrative of romantic love, although my reading of the film does not accept such an ordinary love story. I am not the only one who finds it difficult to accept the movie's basic premise of heterosexual bliss at face value:

Romantic sexuality, so Bonnie thinks, is a way out of ennui. And it is precisely this illusion which is ironically perpetuated by Clyde's impotence. Thanks to the mythology of our time, the viewer is led to believe with Bonnie that if only the couple could have intercourse, all their other troubles would disappear. (Murray, 1978: 154)

Because Bonnie is female and Clyde male, the filmmakers found it difficult to break out of the mold of the heterosexual relationship, union, and consummation; instead, they bent and twisted the tale so it would fit some perceived societal norm. The audience, however, never was and never is fooled into believing in Clyde's impotence.[2] Get real! Handsome Beatty and "knockout" Dunaway must seal their love with sex. A queer reading can enrich our understanding of the subversive potential embedded in *Bonnie and Clyde* and to show how the creation of an alternative family structure among the gang members in the film mirrors the alternative families that queers are forming as an integral part of modern queer culture. Through this lens, the Bonnie-Clyde-C. W. triad is seen as a family unit rather than as a business partnership.

But there is more. I believe that conventional readings of the film, by focusing on the violence in *Bonnie and Clyde*, miss the way in which the level of its cinematic violence is heightened precisely to turn attention away from a diminished level of screen sex. Thus, by seeing the protagonists as outsiders only in terms of crime, viewers fail to see the broader canvas of social protest; similarly, by seeing the action only within the framework of romantic love, viewers miss the restructuring of the family, mirrored in the film, that is a key element of queer culture. This is why I believe it is imperative to offer an alternative analysis of the interplay between sex (even as sexual impotence) and violence (including the phallic gun symbolism). Moreover, as I will show, Clyde comes to see Bonnie not as idealized Woman but as the particular woman who captures his essence in verse. They are soulmates, deeply committed to each other without performing the stereotypical gender roles. This is queer theory in practice.

The path for such an approach to the film is difficult, however, because the screen is a minefield of false clues. With their
with-it style and sense of fashion and flair, Faye Dunaway and
Warren Beatty played Bonnie and Clyde as wannabe movie stars
– an ironic stance because *Bonnie and Clyde* marked Dunaway's
own film debut and Beatty repeats here mannerisms he displayed as the handsome but vacuous jock in *Splendor in the Grass*
(1961), which had been his screen debut. More ironic still is that
Beatty had been handpicked to star in *Splendor* by its homosexual screenwriter, William Inge, who had worked with Beatty
earlier on one of Inge's stage plays. Beatty was already famous as
the red-hot lover of many women; he displayed an aw-shucks
pretty boy demeanor that obviously appealed to gay men and
possibly scared the young actor immensely.

So I think it is important that we examine the reasons for the
change in the screenplay from the erotic homoerotic to the or-
dinarily heterosexual. I will demonstrate that the blasé homosexual was replaced by the tortured impotent man and that the
heterosexual family was replaced by the gang. Moreover, because
research into the ways in which race, class, and gender intersect
and interrelate is gaining prominence in many fields of scholarship, I will highlight those scenes in the film in which African-
American men have been inserted into the narrative as a Greek
chorus, not for verisimilitude, but for showcasing the filmmakers' liberal politics and their commitment to the progressive sixties values of civil rights and racial harmony, both of which had
been missing during the Depression years.

QUEER THEORY, STRANGE THEORY

Paul Julien Smith begins *Laws of Desire*, his book on
homosexuality in Spanish-language writing and film, by asking,
"Is homosexuality a discursive position or a personal identity? Is
it constructed by and in history or is it relatively autonomous of
the social formations within which it is expressed?" (14), and he

ends by positing that there is "no future in attempting to pre-
serve a uniquely homosexual cultural territory, if ever one existed" (214). I think the same can be said for all queer theory:
that it does not make clear what its message might be, and that
perhaps queer space itself is not detectable, dissectable, and dis-
cussable as "a uniquely homosexual cultural territory."

So what does "queer" mean anyway, in connection with theory? Queer theory practitioners are the first to admit that the
term "queer theory" is so new as to be extremely fluid. According to Teresa de Lauretis, "queer" came to displace "lesbian and
gay" in 1990, during a conference at the University of California,
Santa Cruz, because it became evident that "lesbian" and "gay"
were not Siamese twins, but distinct gendered entities. In her
introduction to a special issue of *differences* devoted to queer
theory, she wrote: "In a sense, the term 'Queer Theory' was
arrived at in the effort to avoid all these fine distinctions in our
discursive protocols, not to adhere to any one of the given terms,
not to assume their ideological liabilities, but instead to both
transgress and transcend them – or at the very least problematize
them" (1991: v).

Generally, this new field is used to challenge binary taxono-
mies such as gender, sex, and sexuality and to posit, instead,
continuum categories such as performativity and politics. Performativity refers to the role rather than to the identity of the
performer: a man can perform "female" and a woman can perform "male" since, unlike sex, which is biologically determined,
gender is a role that is as constructed as any theatrical role.[3] In
fact, in Shakespeare's plays during the Elizabethan era, as well
as in traditional Japanese Kabuki theater and in Chinese opera,
all the roles, even the female roles, are played by men who are
judged for their gender performance. Since it was no secret that
the "women" on stage were fictions based on theatrical stereo-
types and conventions of that gender (and of all gender roles),
the criterion was not whether the actors passed as "real"
women, but whether they were convincing in their roles of
"women."

I would like to define "queer" as many do, as anything that is not heterosexist or homophobic, as anything that challenges and interrogates "straight" readings of texts (including the visual arts) and, indeed, of the world. This approach is not without politics, of course: "This does not mean the queerness one attributes to mass culture texts is any less real than the straightness others would claim for these same texts. . . . Queer readings aren't 'alternative' readings. They result from the recognition and articulation of the complex range of queerness that has been in popular culture texts and their audiences all along" (Doty, 1993: xi, 16).

Although there has not yet been a specific queer reading of *Bonnie and Clyde*, there is a growing body of work about queer approaches to film theory (and to cultural theory in general).[4] A queer reading of a work recognizes that intentionally or not the artist explores sexuality and relationships in open-ended ways. Thus "queer" does not represent a binary dichotomy, but an inclusive noncategory capable of embracing myriad forms and objects of desire and discussion.

From the newspaper coverage of Bonnie Parker and Clyde Barrow, the 1930s gangsters, to the myth of Bonnie and Clyde, the 1960s antiheroes, one narrative tool has remained: the love story. The pair have been mated forever despite historical evidence to the contrary. To frame Bonnie and Clyde as undying lovers in crime reinforces the very norms they sought to challenge by living consciously outside the law. Bonnie and Clyde, in real life and in the movies, were outsiders but not outcasts. They chose to live on the fringe, on their own terms. Bonnie and Clyde actively changed the way America perceived them by sending posed photos and autodocumentaries in verse to the media, which published them to the awed delight of readers in the dozen states through which the couple sped while on their two-year robbing and killing spree. While millions of Americans who failed to meet payments were having their homes and farms foreclosed by banks, Depression-era gangsters, such as Bonnie and Clyde, were robbing those banks, and the sense that these otherwise transgressive gangsters were to be admired for their audacity, bravado, and style was widespread.

These gangsters were the first American antiheroes: regular folk who had found a regular job when others could find none. The job may have been to regularly rob banks, but banks during the Depression must have often been seen by the rural unemployed as police are seen today by inner-city unemployed: as untrustworthy and mean, sticking up for the rich against the poor and cutting the underprivileged no slack in their search for a life. It is not surprising, then, to learn that tens of thousands of ordinary men and women flocked to the funerals of such bank robbers when they died, inevitably the victims of gunfire. In the case of Bonnie and Clyde, as reported by the Associated Press the day after their deaths (May 24, 1934), the number of bullets fired at them "as they sped over a Louisiana road at eighty-five miles an hour," was 167.

SEX, VIOLENCE, AND SUBVERSION

If in the 1930s and 1940s, considered by many to be the heyday of Hollywood, the gangster was always a despicable villain who evoked the audience's loathing and disapproval, by 1967, when Arthur Penn's *Bonnie and Clyde* opened, the era of big-screen, full-color antiheroes, of villains who nevertheless win the audience's love and admiration, had begun. Penn portrayed Bonnie and Clyde as stylish, gorgeous, charming young people with lots of energy and drive. Thus, the audience perceived the duo's violence as self-defense and the police search for them as intrusive and petty: couldn't the authorities just let these fabulous people alone? The close-up, realistic slaughter of Bonnie and Clyde at the end of the movie aroused the audience's indignation, revulsion, and shock: how could two people as beautiful as Faye Dunaway and Warren Beatty be so utterly deformed in front of their fans' eyes? The 1967 audience considered the end-of-film slaughter scene, rather than, say, the murder of the bank clerk, shot from within the getaway car after the first robbery, to be the greatest act of transgression depicted in the film.

But today, I think that there are two transgressions in this film that are far more devastating for a queer gaze: the offhand erasure of the homosexual and the overt insertion of African-Americans. So I will begin my queer reading of Arthur Penn's *Bonnie and Clyde* by noting some of the differences between the version of David Newman and Robert Benton's screenplay published in 1986 in Sam Thomas's *Best American Screenplays* and the actual celluloid version (the final shooting script).

These differences begin with the cast of characters that precedes the action: C. W. Moss, an amalgamation of five drivers for the Barrow gang, is described as a "1931 version of a rock-'n'-roll hood; blond, surly, and not very bright" (Thomas, p 253). As the screenwriter David Newman told Vito Russo, author of *The Celluloid Closet*, the first book to examine homosexuality in film:

> In our research we came across references which suggested that several of these guys had been in a sexual thrall with Bonnie and Clyde. So in our first draft that seemed just one more thing which made them outside the structure of society. In fact, in the original draft, there was a shot of the three of them lying in bed together after having sex. . . . Plus, when Michael J. Pollard came along and his character was created, there was no sexuality at all because the part was written especially for him. (135)

In a telephone conversation on November 21, 1995, Newman told me: "We'd come across the fact that some of those guys [drivers] were there also to provide stud services, and speculation that Clyde, in jail, became at least bisexual. We thought this was cool, interesting. It was the sixties. This was before Stonewall, there was no gay sensibility." Newman and Benton thought a homoerotic angle would be "a neat thing" that would add "something different" to the film. The two friends, both writers for glossy *Esquire* magazine, had conducted such "voluminous research" on the gang that they had to "throw out" a lot of material when writing the first version of their screenplay. They dreamed that Clyde would be played by Ben Gazzara, that Jean Seberg would play Bonnie and Gary Crosby C. W. "That was the look we had in our mind. We felt it was making a statement about the sixties underground. Bonnie and Clyde were ahead of their time and thus appealed to us."

Newman and Benton asked a popular French New Wave director, François Truffaut, to direct the film, but he declined, although he offered them useful suggestions. They all agreed that the film's style would be its ultimate appeal. "One of the points to the movie is two people who are stylistically outrageous [although] they were remarkably unsuccessful career criminals. Fascinating. They took pictures of each other and sent them to the papers and had their doggerel published. The Andy Warhol crowd of fifteen minutes of fame, pre *People* magazine. People self-creating their celebrity – appealed to us."

So how did homoeroticism get written out of a project in which celebrity and style – clear cultural codes for queer sensibility – were paramount? How did violence come to supplant sex? According to Russo:

> When Penn and Beatty came on the scene, this aspect of the story [homosexuality] became a liability instead of an interesting asset. Beatty, it was decided, could play an impotent killer but not a sexually ambiguous one and still retain the audience's sympathy. Clyde's "problem" thus became the impotence that Bonnie Parker "cures" in a tender scene in the grass just before the final bloodbath. (135)

By their own admission, then, the filmmakers did not have a very high opinion of their audience, nor of their stars: Beatty was judged too beautiful to be gay, and Pollard was deemed too ugly to be sexual. Both premises were wrong, as this queer critique aims to show. As Rafael Perez-Torres has noted, "Homosexual and heterosexual practices meet in the outlaw to form an irresolvable tension" (205).

Few audiences and critics in 1967 sensed the film's queer subtext, although it was no secret that Newman and Benton had plugged into the rising tide of homosexual sensibility in New York's Greenwich Village for their style. In fact, the movie was released just two years before the Stonewall uprising, that watershed event in the modern Gay and Lesbian Liberation movement.[5] *The New Yorker*'s Pauline Kael wrote perceptively at the time:

> Probably part of the discomfort that people feel about *Bonnie and Clyde* grows out of its compromises and its failures. I wish that the script hadn't provided the upbeat of the hero's sexual success as a kind of sop to the audience. I think what makes us not believe in it is that it isn't consistent with the intelligence of the rest of the writing – that it isn't on the same level, because it's too manipulatively clever, too much of a gimmick. (The scene that shows the gnomish gang member called C. W. sleeping in the same room with Bonnie and Clyde suggests other possibilities, perhaps discarded, as does C. W.'s reference to Bonnie's liking his tattoo.) (47)

The scene in which C. W. proudly shows off the flamboyant tattoo that Bonnie picked out for him is a clear cultural clue for reading the transgressive subtext of the film. After all, in the United States the tattoo is a coded marker for subversion, criminality, violence, and sexuality. In 1933, a year before Bonnie and Clyde were killed, Albert Parry published *Tattoo: Secrets of a Strange Art*, in which he declared that "the very process of tattooing is essentially sexual" (2). Once favored almost exclusively by sailors and soldiers, circus people and criminals, tattoos today are increasingly read as signs of independence and defiance, an integral part of an increasingly in-your-face youth culture.[6] The tattoo, like piercing, is so ubiquitous as to be almost invisible; it is no longer a social signifier of wantonness, violence, and perversion. Even celebrities have tattoos and pose with them proudly for the cameras. The once ominously significant tattoo is no longer a powerful symbol of evil in a world in which uncontextualized random massacres bombard us as we watch television.

It was not always thus. In 1967, before local and global violence began to visit almost every home almost every day through the nightly news, the reviewers of *Bonnie and Clyde* placed the greatest emphasis on the film's violence, the likes of which had never before been shown in commercially released films. Their reviews, compiled in the National Society of Film Critics' *Film 67/68*, include Joseph Morgenstern's categorical dismissal of the film as featuring "some of the most gruesome carnage since Verdun" (25), followed publicly a week later by his revised evaluation that "violent movies are an inevitable consequence of violent life" (27); John Simon's analysis, which has formed the basis for many subsequent volumes about violence in film, that "the film's aestheticizing continually obtrudes on and obfuscates moral values" (32); and, finally, Kael's already-mentioned essay, which helped establish her reputation: "The brutality that comes out of this innocence is far more shocking than the calculated brutalities of mean killers" (45).

But although violence was considered the overwhelming transgression of the film, others were also noted. For example, Peter Collier commented scathingly, in the influential left-wing journal *Ramparts*, on the film's stylish "pop nihilism":

> The movie doesn't have much to do with the dumpy, putty-faced dame who was Bonnie Parker, or with the homosexual punk who was Clyde Barrow. It doesn't have much to do with the world these two pillaged. . . . The two glamorous desperados – a whole Capote party in themselves – have found that their new life, which began so intensely, will be flittered away. . . . They were an advertiser's dream the minute they were reborn. Every new life style has a built-in con, from which it is only a short step to a racket. (22)

Collier's rage, although warranted by the Vietnam War era's politics of personal engagement and responsibility, unfortunately sideswipes some deeper issues, ones to which Kael is surprisingly attuned, namely, the film's sexual and social transgressions.

QUEER READING, QUEER PERFORMANCES

To me, key scenes in the film indicate a queer sensibility. Such a queer reading involves the realization that gender, like any role, is a performance: actors play many roles, including all the ones they can imagine and create along the male-female continuum. It is interesting to observe how impotently Bonnie plays the savvy seductress and, conversely, with what gusto Clyde plays the impotent macho:

> Because many men are forced to comply with macho standards of performance, standards frequently reinforced . . . they experience their power and sexuality as heavy burdens. By adopting a model of sexuality and social relations that is neither hierarchical nor exploitative, men can begin to construct alternative relationships among themselves as well as with women. (Murphy, 1994: 4)

One important scene, mentioned by Kael earlier, blatantly focuses on the puzzled, anguished look on Bonnie's face as she is caught in a hotel room, at night, between the snoring of either C. W. or Clyde. Is this the scene written to replace Bonnie and Clyde's threesome situation with the blond hunk, a scene cut from the original screenplay? Probably, especially when we later see C. W. scamper outside in his long johns to meet Clyde's newlywed brother, Buck, and his wife, Blanche, in their car.

Another queer scene occurs about forty-four minutes into the film, when Bonnie, C. W., Clyde, Buck, and Blanche all check into a rental property together, ready to settle down for a short while and play house. We, the viewers, have already seen that whereas Clyde and Buck are close and chummy, Bonnie and Blanche are cool and aloof toward each other. Each woman obviously has a very definite and deadly opinions about the other. We have also noticed that the newly married Buck and Blanche are sexually attracted to each other and that the "lovers," Bonnie and Clyde, are not. In this pivotal scene between life on the lam and life at home, we see Blanche go to the refrigerator, open it, and gasp from the stench of rotted food. The camera then registers the bored Bonnie, with whom we look on as Clyde brings a heavy box of ammunition in from the car and almost drops with it to the floor. We see Clyde walk right past Bonnie without noticing her desire for assurance and warmth. He comes up to C. W. and offers him a lick of his ice cream stick, surely an obvious sign of affection, if not lust.

Such critical clues that something besides robbing banks together is going on between Clyde and C. W. are scattered throughout the film, but each is so fleetingly displayed that it seems more like a subliminal message than an actual film cue. Nevertheless, this short scene is so erotically charged that I cannot understand how it survived the cutting room. Yet not only does this scene make it into the film's final cut, but the scene dissolves into an even more explicit one that shows everyone relaxed and content except for the petulantly smoking Bonnie.

Everyone is settling into the homey space. But watch carefully as the camera invites us into the checkers game. As we "read" the screen, we see that to the left of the checkers board the always flirting and playful Buck and Blanche are locked in an embrace, while to the right of the checkers board is the squatting C. W. And we cannot fail to notice Clyde, hugging C. W. in an enveloping embrace from behind. The two men seem to be almost cuddling: in a conventional reading, this would clearly be a counterpoint critique of the juxtaposition between this couple and the heterosexual one on the sofa. Throughout this brief scene we notice Bonnie, neglected, sitting hurt and sullen in a mid-screen chair directly in front of our eyes. She clearly understands what is happening, even if the critics do not, and she is not amused.

Bonnie still has the clout to signal Clyde that she must talk to him privately. They repair to their bedroom, where she taunts him about Blanche and Buck. Changing her demeanor once more to that of a concerned, petulant, scorned lover, Bonnie then asks Clyde whether he ever feels like being alone with her. Clyde, baffled and cagey, replies that he does feel that they are alone when they are together. He smiles nervously, proceeds to say that he is hungry, and leaves Bonnie as the picture dissolves. It is this scene that can remind the careful viewer of a telling detail from one of Bonnie and Clyde's first encounters in the movie. Bonnie is sitting in a car that Clyde had stolen while Clyde, standing outside but placing his head inside the car through the open window, admits to not being a "lover boy." Clyde then adds that he is not, however, attracted to men – at which point, like the wooden Pinocchio whose nose grew with every lie, he bumps his head on the car.

Such scenes were not meant to convey the homoeroticism that they so strongly do. Despite their every effort to achieve the contrary, despite the rewrites and the reshoots, the filmmakers could not erase the original screenplay. Am I seeing things because of some queer agenda? Not at all, as can be gauged from Dunaway's autobiography, *Looking for Gatsby*:

> An early draft of the script had Clyde, Bonnie, and C. W. in a love triangle. Bonnie was a nymphomaniac, Clyde was a homosexual, and C. W. was in the middle of it all. It was a subplot that had the potential to overtake the rest of the story as it stood. As the script evolved, that piece of the story largely disappeared. There are brief scenes that survived that hint of what might have been more than just a boss-and-sidekick relationship between C. W. and Clyde. During one, the gang is passing time in a roadside motel, and C. W. and Buck are playing checkers, with Clyde showing C. W. how to play. There is a familiar intimacy between the two men that speaks

of something deeper. . . . In movies, it's boy meets girl, and they live happily ever after. But we were trying to do something new and modern with this relationship, which was to say, "Look, the guy is practically impotent," which also happens to have been the truth. (129)

The clues were there on the set, and they are in the final cut as well. Clyde may be no red-hot lover, but when he is attracted to others he is not particularly choosy about their gender; he is an egalitarian rogue. This may explain why, although it is standard fare for cinematic criminals to kill each other for incompetence, perceived or real, Clyde does not terminate C. W. after their botched getaway. You will remember that Bonnie and Clyde had just robbed a bank and killed a pursuing banker who had jumped into the windshield of the slowly departing getaway car C. W. was erratically driving.

The trio escapes their pursuers by using the standard cinematic ploy of ducking into a darkened theater while a movie is in progress (films have been self-referential from the beginning). The movie is *Gold Diggers of 1933*, the story of showgirls trying to help a producer open a musical during the Depression so that they may all be able to pay the rent and buy food to eat. Bonnie is enraptured by the movie magic of the contextually ironic, over-the-top production number "We're in the Money." She clearly identifies with the chorus girls who want to be wrapped in mink. Later, she sings a few bars while preening in front of the mirror in yet another musty motel.

Meanwhile, Clyde, sitting apart from Bonnie, berates C. W. while hitting him over the head with his cap. Clyde's frustration, however, never turns into violence against the youth; he is family. Viewers in 1967 were taught to expect retribution for failure in gangster movies, so they were unprepared for this new twist. The family theme is replayed during the Parker family reunion half an hour later in the film. The audience is regaled with yet another glimpse of the tenderness between Clyde and C. W., who is clearly accepted as a member of the extended Parker clan.

In the midst of the scene, while Bonnie rolls in the sand and the young children frolic, Clyde walks up the hillock where C. W. stands guard to relieve him of his rifle. Clyde tucks a napkin under C. W.'s chin and gives him some food to eat. The two men stand together, smiling contentedly in the warm sun.

Such a sweet gesture could be excused as charmingly familial rather than be interpreted as highly eroticized were the viewers not already conditioned by the filmmakers always to be aware of the cinematic sublimation of sexual desire into cool firearms. Careful viewers will recall that when Bonnie first meets Clyde he lets her fondle his gun. Later, after he tells Bonnie that he is impotent, he shows off his firepower by robbing a store. Because food and firearms express repressed sexuality in this movie, it is interesting that both these subliminal subtexts are used to link Clyde with Bonnie as well as with C. W. – especially because the filmmakers consciously tried to hide the latter connection from viewers by emphasizing violence and romantic love.

John Cawelti, whose *Focus on "Bonnie and Clyde"* has become a classic critical collection, writes about the perceived romantic center of the film, stating: "it is primarily through her developing love for Clyde that Bonnie reaches the level of recognition and awareness that gives her a tragic dignity in the fatal culmination of her flight from the tawdry room and the hopeless trap of her job as a waitress in a cheap café" (48). This analysis, although overlooking the historical facts – Bonnie was married to another; Clyde was a sociopath with no ability to form a loving relationship – does offer a refreshing approach:

> At first, her interest in Clyde seems largely sexual; unlike the other men who are continually pawing at her, Clyde, with his air of impulsive spontaneity and his potent gun, seems to offer a liberating sexual exhilaration. However, when she discovers that Clyde is impotent, instead of leaving, she accepts his fantasy of power and fame. Precisely because she recognizes her need for the self-image that Clyde offers her, Bonnie is forced to an initial realization of the difference between love as sexual aggression and love as mutual response and support (49).

The "potent gun" motif is not unique; it is found in most critiques of the film. As Robert Kolker notes, "Bonnie caresses his gun and urges him to 'use it,' pressing the connection between repressed sexuality and the need for some physical action in which to sublimate it" (34). Edward Murray, who lists *Bonnie and Clyde* as one of his *Ten Film Classics*, adds: "At the beginning of the film, Bonnie's mouth is shown half-opened with desire for something she cannot even name. But in our society, the first thing her lips come in contact with is Coca Cola" (152). And, I may add, we can watch Clyde's lips twirl an unlit wooden match, which acts like a surrogate/subliminal/excited penis throughout the film, and Bonnie's always mesmerized gaze at Clyde's unholstered gun.

If sex is the longing, violence is the act. The sociopath confuses satisfaction through violence with satisfaction from sex. After all, it is easier to establish a relationship with a gun than with a person; guns are easier to control. Clyde's film impotence is compensated for by his shooting and driving expertise: Clyde may be impotent, but he is handsome, strong, and energetic; Bonnie may have a sex urge, but violence is a powerful substitute for physical passion.

By the time Penn shot *Bonnie and Clyde*, the studio system was crumbling and, with it, the strictures of the Hays Code of on-screen morality (1930–66). In the midst of the war waged by the underground press against censorship and for the most permissive interpretation of the First Amendment, extending its guaranty of the right of free speech to protect free depiction as well, Penn chose to depict graphic violence rather than homoerotic sexuality. This conscious commercial choice compromises the film's integrity.

Although it is set in the thirties, *Bonnie and Clyde* is a self-consciously sixties film. The 1960s were confusing times for choices; as Meredith Cry notes in another context: "When a society has lost confidence in its own values and in its ability to enforce its views, optimistic individuals may think of it as being less restricted, rather than as breaking down" (241). *Bonnie and*

Clyde, while full of vim and vigor, of stunning style and madcap action, misses becoming a socially aware film despite its attempts to paint itself in that light; ultimately, the film takes fewer risks than it can. Take the sex, so tame despite the demise of the moral code:

> For years [compliance with code] had meant coy use of sheets, separate beds even for married couples, and passionate embraces that faded to long shots of flames licking at logs in fireplaces, thunderstorms with phallic bolts of lightning, long trains entering dark tunnels, and restless surf pounding rhythmically against rocky coasts. Such sly metaphors did not fit the swinging Sixties or the let-it-all-hang-out mood of the early Seventies. In an era of massage parlors and nude encounter groups, audiences were curious, yellow and blue, and craved greater realism . . . the code managed to stretch enough to allow . . . slow-motion violence in *Bonnie and Clyde*. (Keyser, 1981: 53)

Disingenuously, Penn kept to the no-sex sections of the code while gleefully adding to the level of visceral, visual violence; the sex was linked to the violence through the erotic fetishization of the violence. Penn's strategy worked. For most audiences, critics, and reviewers, *Bonnie and Clyde* has remained one of the best, most influential, and oft-quoted films of the sixties.[7]

Douglas Brode writes that Penn "explored the relationship of sex and violence in society by concentrating on the shifting relationships between the characters." Clyde is impotent, preferring guns to sex with Bonnie, but after Bonnie and Clyde make love, "they kill no one else. . . . Sex and violence are seen as the positive and negative aspects of a single force: when one is repressed, the other is released in devastating proportions" (204). But this potential for examining the yin and yang of sex and violence, expression and repression, is never explored, except in the most mundane way: sex is redemptive; violence is phallic; a circular dance that is never challenged. Penn wanted to make a statement about the perils of the excessive use of force and violence, but the cinematic carnage was received with such reverent shock that it has spawned ever bloodier clones: "Film is not innocent, not *merely* entertainment, and most especially not divorced from the culture out of which it comes and into which it feeds. . . . Form took precedence over meaning, and the formal trend of violence started with *Bonnie and Clyde* has been irresistible" (Kolker, 14, 57).

Cinematic change is gingerly meted out in small doses; the dictum of giving the audience what it wants is still supreme, and nobody argues with success. As Man notes:

> By a process of association, *Bonnie and Clyde* appealed to a whole generation of moviegoers infected by its own anti-establishment zeitgeist in the 1960s. . . . When Bonnie and Clyde die up there on the screen, something dies in us as well – that spark that enabled us to identify with them in the first place and of which they were an expression – a breath of imagination, an expansiveness of spirit that we deny ourselves in our conventional existence. That is why the depiction of their death is so crucial, for it must reimburse us for our emotional investment in the lives of these characters. (29–30)

However, *Bonnie and Clyde* is quite subversive on a purely cinematic level. The film flaunts conventions. As Kolker reminds us, the balletic deaths of Bonnie and Clyde are a deviation from both film convention and the original script: "With *Bonnie and Clyde*, Penn breaks for good and all a major cinematic contract between viewer and filmmaker which held that violent death on the screen would be swift and relatively clean" (49). Before body bags littered American living rooms nightly, Penn showed the way: "*Bonnie and Clyde* opened the bloodgates, and our cinema has barely stopped bleeding since" (52).

More daring still, Penn breaks the unwritten contract with the viewers by starting the film without an establishing shot. We first catch a glimpse of Bonnie's lips, then a series of claustrophobic images of Bonnie on her bed and in her bedroom, presumed but not shown to be naked. Only after nine minutes of film, after Clyde performs an armed robbery to impress Bonnie and

FIGURE 30
The potent gun motif: repressed sexuality intimately connected
to physical violence.

they make their first joint getaway, do they finally introduce
themselves to each other – and, to the viewers.

So although *Bonnie and Clyde* flamboyantly flaunts convention, it retains the untampered scenario of true love, basic to
every broad-on-the-road movie. Unwilling to explore the complex relationship between Bonnie and Clyde, the film presents
them as two-dimensional characters: "Frustrated inhabitants of
a society which makes responsible adulthood difficult to come
by, and which denies satisfaction of basic human and spiritual
desires, Bonnie and Clyde are doomed victims of arrested development" (Murray, 152).

In the end, *Bonnie and Clyde* subverts easy identification with
the heterosexual universe despite the filmmakers' best heterosex-

ist intentions. Even the "cure" of Clyde's impotence is left in limbo as a subliminal suggestion rather than proven. By the late sixties, the women's movement had already made public the existence of the false faked female orgasm, whereby a woman would provide the appropriate sounds to accompany her lover's sexual performance. Thus, the heterosexual lovemaking pastiched onto *Bonnie and Clyde* is as unsatisfying to the average viewer today as it was for the astute Pauline Kael nearly thirty-odd years ago. For current viewers, as well as for many queer theorists, sexual performance is largely irrelevant; sensual pleasure can be achieved in many other ways as well. In the final analysis, what Clyde discovers in Bonnie's arms is not sexual potency but binding intimacy.

Ironically, the exhilarating gender subversion of the film is unplanned. Because Clyde is portrayed as sexually impotent, Bonnie ultimately transcends her situation as small-town waitress, using not her body but her brain. By erasing the homosexual without omitting the queer perception of interpersonal relationships, Penn created a movie that I can define only as queer. In *Bonnie and Clyde*, queerness is portrayed as much more than mere sexual orientation; it is a way of life. This approach is quintessentially queer, opening rather than closing possibilities of interaction.

The historical evidence is clear: Clyde was homosexual, and Bonnie was married to another gangster, conveniently in jail. John Treherne, after exhaustively researching the lives of the legendary duo, concludes:

> Clyde Barrow was evidently an undemonstrative lover. . . .
> [An] acquaintance remarked that "Clyde had a mistrust of any woman except Bonnie." Whatever his sexual limitation, Clyde Barrow had plainly kindled something in Bonnie's quick impressionable nature that made her see criminals not as sordid clowns but as glamorous adventurers. . . . Perhaps the violence and weaponry of criminal violence also stirred deeper, physical levels of her love for Clyde as it did for some of her Hollywood counterparts (93).

Peter Wollen notes that any semiotic approach to film analysis must include "the *secret*" – which he identifies as the search for "desired knowledge" (40). Although Wollen's analysis works best in the mystery genre, I think it works quite well in ferreting out the queer elements in the film, submerged as they may be, because queer sexuality is the ultimate *secret* in straight society. As Jonathan Goldberg comments, "Homosexuality is . . . the secret inside of heterosexuality" (80). Finally, as Carolyn Geduld points out, *Bonnie and Clyde*'s "final critical success depends on the extent to which the psychological motivation of the characters coincides with the larger theme. The return of Clyde's potency, for instance, may be explained as the breaking of an archetypal taboo, but it is not quite believable in terms of the character Warren Beatty creates" (98). The erasure of the queer, then, detracts from the film's subversive strength.

QUEER DOMESTIC SPACE

In the sixties, sons were either shipped to war overseas or crossed a nearer border to escape the draft; working and college women were discovering the sexual revolution thanks to the Pill; hippies were tuning out and reemerging in communes across North America; and social outcasts on society's fringes were encouraged to create alternative families. In this last sense, queers, who had always grouped and regrouped in fluid underground communities, were coming closer to the margins of the mainstream.

The Barrow gang in general, and Bonnie and Clyde in particular, afford us a glimpse into what such an alternative family might be in the thirties, in the sixties and beyond. They are loyal, caring, fun-loving and unconventional. As Clyde tells Bonnie, "I'm your family." Clyde is touched that Bonnie chooses to stay with him despite the danger from the law. When she refuses to leave him and save herself, he is moved to try to make love to her, but cannot. His arms (all of them) provide cold comfort.

Bonnie and Clyde are more like close-knit brother and sister than intimate lovers. But gang propriety forbids incest, and according to Carolyn Geduld:

> Similarly, patricide is so inconceivable within the domestic setting that it must be turned into its opposite. . . . [The men] throw *mock* punches, play checkers, and take each other's photographs. . . . Love and the absence of sexual provocation: these are the elements which keep the family intact. . . . In the end, Bonnie and Clyde die, not because they rob and murder but because they break the archetypal clan taboos and themselves dissolve their domestic solidarity. (95–6)[8]

How was this "domestic solidarity" created in the film? When Bonnie first sees Clyde, he is trying to steal her mother's car – and ten minutes later, Bonnie is leaving her mother, job, and past behind to follow him (and his gun) wherever stolen cars will take them. They have formed a bond. Later, when they meet C. W. Moss, they spontaneously decide to share that space with him. Following another bank robbery, the threesome are joined by Buck and Blanche to form an extended family and begin to play house together.

Not for long, however. The domestic sphere is their undoing. "This is one of the schematic themes," David Newman acknowledged in our conversation. "Every time they try to settle down to a lower-class 'normal' family, they're at their most vulnerable." He added that one of his primary motivations in writing the script had been to show an alternative family structure. (Elsewhere he has written that his favorite movie is *Rio Bravo*, in which another alternative family is created as well.)

Concomitantly, by not daring to tamper with heterosexual norms, Penn almost misses the single most important revolution of the sixties: feminism. Bonnie and Blanche utilize the expanded space created for them by the boyish men and become increasingly forceful and resourceful. If in the first shot we see Bonnie, her lips puckered and pouting while she is pent-up at home, we later see her at home in the wide world, comfortable with notoriety and celebrity, power and poetry. Even stereotypically mousy Blanche starts wearing pants (and carrying a riding crop!) and demanding her share of the spoils. The two women, despising each other at first sight, never allowing the other a real look, finally face each other in a friendly way, as if they had come to a mutual realization of each other's worth as a person.

Finally, another way in which a queer reading can enrich our viewing of *Bonnie and Clyde* is by paying attention to those men the filmmakers chose to insert into the vacuum formed by the erasure of queer: African-Americans. Having rewritten Clyde as impotent, the screenwriters searched for another "neat" way to show their progressive liberal views. It would be their passport to approval with hip audiences, and they found it in their insertion of African-Americans. A pair of African-American men in overalls streak across the screen from time to time, like a Greek chorus delivering a subliminal message of the filmmakers' liberal ethos: they loll on the street; they enter the bank that the pair has just robbed, and so on. At the very end, they arrive in a chicken truck just in time to watch the slaughter of Bonnie and Clyde. The Black duo is used as tropes for a "model minority" and as foils for the "jes' folks" white duo, the Robin Hood–Maid Marion madcap traveling show.

CONCLUSION

I believe that texts and films have a larger cultural meaning and that contextualizing them is important for making the invisible visible and the seeming, real. It is a political act in the way that education is always a political act. Reading and viewing can be equally political acts – acts of survival as well as of subversion, above and below and through the social fabric that informs them.

Missionaries of morals, who sometimes live the lifestyles they preach against, come and go through the cultural landscape. After the media frenzy around the "coming out" episode of ABC's situation comedy *Ellen* on April 30, 1997, it is sobering to remember that we have been there before. As Russo reminds us in *The Celluloid Closet*, "*Time* announced [in June 1968] that 'the third sex' was making a determined bid for first place at the box office" because so many gay-themed plays and movies were being produced (163). What *Time* neglected to mention was that the gay characters invariably died by the final reel, often horribly. There was no positive message about choice and compassion. For Russo, "Violence by and toward homosexuals on screen escalated at the end of the 1960s and became the keynote of the 1970s. Sissies were now cured, killed or rendered impotent in suitably nasty ways" (162).

I am not suggesting that *Bonnie and Clyde*, its original screenplay intact, would have been a harbinger of happier endings, since the protagonists were devoted to each other and deadly to almost everyone else, but that if movies had portrayed a wider range of lesbians, gay men, bisexuals, and transsexuals from the start the public could have been sensitized to a larger canvas of characters. Instead, the public has been screen-fed a convoluted concept of queer that is dehumanizing and wrong.

In the 1940s, Hollywood tackled the social problem film. The first theme, in 1947, after World War II, was anti-Semitism (*Crossfire, Gentleman's Agreement*), which was followed, two years later, by the theme of racism (*Lost Boundaries, Pinky, Home of the Brave*). It is instructive to realize that one of the 1947 films, *Crossfire*, is based on a novel about homophobia, and that one of the 1949 films, *Home of the Brave*, is at its source a play about anti-Semitism. Bigotry has no strict borders; it strikes equally at everyone whom it first dehumanizes. Thus, homophobia is not an isolated case of prejudice and stereotyping, but part and parcel of the way such forces work insidiously to tear society from its roots. To combat bigotry, we must understand how these roots entwine.

Bonnie and Clyde is a fascinating example because it shows how values are warped by insensitive stereotyping, and it rhapsodizes about violence, placing it above other forms of human contact. Hollywood will do well to get beyond its traditional binary poles of love and hate, romance and violence. There are powerful stories to be told about the range of colors all along the prism of life. After a century of cinema, viewers are ready for more sophisticated shades and more complicated characters.

NOTES

I would like to thank Robert Kolker, in whose film seminar I presented an embryonic version of this paper, and Gina Marchetti, for whose cultural criticism seminar I prepared an expanded version, for their guidance, inspiration, and support. Both seminars were held at the University of Maryland College Park in 1995. I would also like to thank my partner, Dr. Susan Kirshner, for critical conversations that helped me to shape and sharpen my thoughts and my writing.

1. In another chapter of this book, Matthew Bernstein suggests, as Vito Russo noted, that the homosexual subtext of the original screenplay did not survive onto the screen, but in this chapter I will show that, in fact, more than its trace has survived into the final cut of the film.

2. Thomas Elaesser writes about the power of nonrepressed sexuality in melodrama thus: "Male impotence and female frigidity is a subject that allows for thematization in various directions, not only to indicate the kinds of psychological anxiety and social pressures that generally make people sexually unresponsive, but as metaphors of a lack of freedom (Hitchcock's frigid heroines) or as quasi-metaphysical 'overarching' (as in [Nicholas] Ray's *Bigger Than Life*). In [Douglas] Sirk, where the theme has an exemplary status, it is treated as a problem of decadence – where intention, awareness, and yearning outstrip sexual, social, and moral performance" (1992: 534).

3. It might be useful to think of sex as hardware and of gender as software: people are hard-wired by their chromosomes, their genes, to be either male or female, but they can insert any software they wish and "play" or "perform" any gender role, since, unlike sex, gender is a fluid, socially constructed category.

4. For example: Bell-Metereau, 1993; Clum, 1992; de Lauretis, 1984; Doty, 1993; Doty and Creekmur, 1995; Dyer 1984; Dyer 1990; Fuss, 1991; Mercer, 1994; Russo, 1987; Tyler, 1972; and Weiss, 1992.

5. On June 27, 1969, the clients of the Stonewall Inn, a Village bar favored by transvestites, retaliated for the first time against the police who habitually came to harass them. The immediate result was three days of riots; the subsequent result was the public genesis of the struggle for gay and lesbian rights. Some have theorized that a major catalyst for the Stonewall uprising was Judy Garland's death earlier that week, for the perennially sad yet plucky singer-actress had been and continues to be a gay icon of against-the-odds perseverance.

6. Parry cites a "significant court decision" in 1920s Boston "recognizing tattooing as, in effect, a voluntary sexual experience" (3). Two rapists were set free (after a brief reprimand) because the teenaged girl had a small butterfly tattoo and was thus deemed a non-virgin; unmarried non-virgins were considered wanton. Tattoos were symbols for sexuality in the 1930s; not surprisingly, after her death, it was discovered that the real-life Bonnie Parker sported a tattoo on her thigh.

7. See Brode, 1980; Cawelti, 1979; Clarens, 1979; Geduld, 1979; Hillier, 1979; Kolker, 1988; Man, 1994; Murray, 1978; Samuels, 1979; Stein, 1995; Thomas, 1986; Treherne, 1985.

8. We have little knowledge about queer culture before the Stonewall uprising in June 1969, although some of the story is emerging through the Lesbian Herstory Archives, other historical projects and films such as Greta Shiller's *Before Stonewall*. "Rumor and gossip constitute the unrecorded history of gay subculture," following Patricia Meyer Spacks's notion of gossip as something that "provides language for an alternative culture. . . . It is this insistence by the dominant culture on making homosexuality invisible and unspeakable in rumor, innuendo, fleeting gestures and coded language" (Weiss, 1992: 30, 32).

WORKS CITED

Bell-Metereau, Rebecca. *Hollywood Androgyny*. 2d ed. New York: Columbia University Press, 1993.

Brode, Douglas. *The Films of the Sixties*. Secaucus, NJ: Citadel Press, 1980.

Cawelti, John G. "The Artistic Power of *Bonnie and Clyde*." In *Focus on "Bonnie and Clyde*," edited by John G. Cawelti, 40–84. Film Focus. Englewood Cliffs, NJ: Prentice-Hall, 1979.

Clarens, Carlos. *Crime Movies*. New York: W. W. Norton, 1979.

Clum, John M. *Acting Gay: Male Homosexuality in Modern Drama. Between Men, Between Women*. New York: Columbia University Press, 1992.

Collier, Peter. "The Barrow Gang: An Aftertaste." *Ramparts*, May 1968: 16–22.

Crimp, Douglas. "Right On, Girlfriend!" In *Fear of a Queer Planet*. Edited by Michael Warner, 300–20. Minneapolis: University of Minnesota Press, 1993.

Cry, Meredith. *Different Drummers: A Study of Cultural Alternatives in Fiction*. Metuchen, NJ: Scarecrow Press, 1984.

de Lauretis, Teresa. *Alice Doesn't: Feminism, Semiotics, Cinema*. Bloomington: Indiana University Press, 1984.

    "Introduction." *differences* 3.2 (1991): iii–xviii.

Doty, Alexander. *Making Things Perfectly Queer: Interpreting Mass Culture*. Minneapolis: University of Minnesota Press, 1993.

Doty, Alexander, and Corey K. Creekmur, eds. *Out in Culture: Gay, Lesbian, and Queer Essays on Popular Culture*. Durham, NC: Duke University Press, 1995.

Dunaway, Faye, with Betsy Sharkey. *Looking for Gatsby*. New York: Simon and Schuster, 1995.

Dyer, Richard. *Now You See It*. London and New York: Routledge, 1990.

Dyer, Richard, ed. *Gays and Film*. New York: Zoetrope, 1984.

Elsaesser, Thomas. "Tales of Sound and Fury: Observations on the Family Melodrama." In *Film Theory and Criticism*, 4th ed., edited by Gerald Mast, Marshall Cohen, and Leo Braudy, 512–35. New York and Oxford: Oxford University Press, 1992.

Fuss, Diana, ed. *inside/out: Lesbian Theories, Gay Theories*. New York: Routledge, 1991.

Geduld, Carolyn. "*Bonnie and Clyde:* Society vs. the Clan." In *Focus*, ed. Cawelti, 93–8.

Goldberg, Jonathan. "Sodometries." In *English Inside and Out*, edited by Susan Gubar and Jonathan Kamholtz, 68–86. New York: Routledge, 1993.

Hillier, Jim. "Arthur Penn." In *Focus*, ed. Cawelti, 7–14.

Kael, Pauline. "Bonnie and Clyde." In *Film 67/68*, 46–48. New York: Simon & Schuster, 1968.

Keyser, Les. *Hollywood in the Seventies*. San Diego: A. S. Barnes, 1981.

Kolker, Robert Phillip. *A Cinema of Loneliness: Penn, Kubrick, Scorsese, Spielberg, Altman*. 2d ed. New York: Oxford University Press, 1988.

Man, Glenn. *Radical Visions: American Film Renaissance, 1967–1976*. Contributions to the Study of Popular Culture 41. Westport, Conn.: Greenwood Press, 1994.

Mercer, Kobena. *Welcome to the Jungle: New Positions in Black Cultural Studies*. New York: Routledge, 1994.

Murphy, Peter F. "Introduction." In *Fictions of Masculinity: Crossing Cul-*

tures, *Crossing Sexualities*, edited by Peter F. Murphy, 1–17. New York: New York University Press, 1994.

Murray, Edward. *Ten Film Classics: A Re-Viewing.* Ungar Film Library. New York: Frederick Ungar Publishing Co., 1978.

National Society of Film Critics, ed. *Film 67/68.* New York: Simon and Schuster, 1968.

Parry, Albert. *Tattoo: Secrets of a Strange Art.* 1933. Reprint, New York: Collier Books, 1971.

Perez-Torres, Rafael. "The Ambiguous Outlaw: John Rechy and Complicitous Homotextuality." In *Fictions of Masculinity*, ed. Murphy, 204–25. New York: New York University Press, 1994.

Russo, Vito. *The Celluloid Closet: Homosexuality in the Movies.* Triangle Classics. Rev. ed. New York: Quality Paperback Book Club, 1987.

Samuels, Charles Thomas. "*Bonnie and Clyde.*" In *Focus*, ed. Cawelti, 85–92.

Smith, Paul Julian. *Laws of Desire: Questions of Homosexuality in Spanish Writing and Film, 1960–1990.* Oxford: Clarendon Press, 1992.

Stein, Michael Eric. "The New Violence, or Twenty Years of Violence in Films: An Appreciation (Part I)." *Films in Review*, January/February 1995: 40–9.

Thomas, Sam, ed. *Best American Screenplays.* New York: Crown Publishers, 1986.

Treherne, John. *The Strange History of Bonnie and Clyde.* New York: Stein and Day, 1985.

Tyler, Parker. *Screening the Sexes: Homosexuality in the Movies.* New York: Holt, Rinehart and Winston, 1972.

Weiss, Andrea. *Vampires and Violets: Lesbians in the Cinema.* London: Jonathan Cape, 1992.

Wollen, Peter. *Readings and Writings: Semiotic Counter-Strategies.* London: Verso, 1982.

Reviews of *Bonnie and Clyde*

BONNIE AND CLYDE ARRIVES

BOSLEY CROWTHER

Reprinted from *The New York Times*, August 14, 1967.

A raw and unmitigated campaign of sheer pressagentry has been trying to put across the notion that Warner Brothers' "Bonnie and Clyde" is a faithful representation of the desperado careers of Clyde Barrow and Bonnie Parker, a notorious team of bank robbers and killers who roamed Texas and Oklahoma in the post-Depression years.

It is nothing of the sort. It is a cheap piece of bald-faced slapstick comedy that treats the hideous depredations of that sleazy, moronic pair as though they were as full of fun and frolic as the jazz-age cut-ups in "Thoroughly Modern Millie." And it puts forth Warren Beatty and Faye Dunaway in the leading roles, and Michael J. Pollard as their sidekick, a simpering, nose-picking rube, as though they were striving mightily to be the Beverly Hillbillies of next year.

It has Mr. Beatty clowning broadly as the killer who fondles various types of guns with as much nonchalance and dispassion as he airily twirls a big cigar, and it has Miss Dunaway squirming grossly as his thrill-seeking, sex-starved moll. It is loaded with farcical holdups, screaming chases in stolen getaway cars that have the antique appearance and speeded-up movement of the clumsy vehicles of the Keystone Cops, and indications of the impotence of Barrow, until Bonnie writes a poem about him to extol his prowess, that are as ludicrous as they are crude.

Such ridiculous, camp-tinctured travesties of the kind of people these desperados were and of the way people lived in the dusty Southwest back in those barren years might be passed off as candidly commercial movie comedy, nothing more, if the film weren't reddened with blotches of violence of the most grisly sort.

Arthur Penn, the aggressive director, has evidently gone out of his way to splash the comedy holdups with smears of vivid blood as astonished people are machine-gunned. And he has staged the terminal scene of the ambuscading and killing of Barrow and Bonnie by a posse of policemen with as much noise and gore as is in the climax of "The St. Valentine's Day Massacre."

This blending of farce with brutal killings is as pointless as it is lacking in taste, since it makes no valid commentary upon the already travestied truth. And it leaves an astonished critic wondering just what purpose Mr. Penn and Mr. Beatty think they serve with this strangely antique, sentimental claptrap, which opened yesterday at the Forum and the Murray Hill.

This is the film that opened the Montreal International Festival!

━━━━━━━━━━━━━━

BONNIE AND CLYDE

PAULINE KAEL

Reprinted from Pauline Kael, *For Keeps* (New York: Plume, 1994), 141–57. Originally published in *The New Yorker*, October 21, 1967.

How do you make a good movie in this country without being jumped on? *Bonnie and Clyde* is the most excitingly American American movie since *The Manchurian Candidate*. The audience is alive to it. Our experience as we watch it has some connection with the way we reacted to movies in childhood: with how we came to love them and to feel they were ours – not an art that we learned over the years to appreciate but simply and immediately ours. When an American movie is contemporary in feeling, like this one, it makes a different kind of contact with an American audience from the kind that is made by European films, however contemporary. Yet any movie that is contemporary in feeling is likely to go further than other movies – go too far for some tastes – and *Bonnie and Clyde* divides audiences, as *The Manchurian Candidate* did, and it is being jumped on almost as hard. Though we may dismiss the attacks with "What good movie doesn't give some offense?," the fact that it is generally *only* good movies that provoke attacks by many people suggests that the innocuousness of most of our movies is accepted with such complacence that when an American movie reaches people, when it makes them react, some of them think there must be something the matter with it – perhaps a law should be passed against it. *Bonnie and Clyde* brings into the almost frighteningly public world of movies things that people have been feeling and saying and writing about. And once something is said or done on the screens of the world, once it has entered mass art, it can never again belong to a minority, never again be the private possession of an educated, or "knowing," group. But even for that group there is an excitement in hearing its own private thoughts expressed out loud and in seeing something of its own sensibility become part of our common culture.

Our best movies have always made entertainment out of the antiheroism of American life; they bring to the surface what, in its newest forms and fashions, is always just below the surface. The romanticism in American movies lies in the cynical tough guy's independence; the sentimentality lies, traditionally, in the falsified finish when the anti-hero turns hero. In 1967, this kind of sentimentality wouldn't work with the audience, and *Bonnie and Clyde* substitutes sexual fulfillment for a change of heart. (This doesn't quite work, either; audiences sophisticated enough to enjoy a movie like this one are too sophisticated for the dramatic uplift of the triumph over impotence.)

Structurally, *Bonnie and Clyde* is a story of love on the run, like the old Clark Gable–Claudette Colbert *It Happened One Night* but turned inside out; the walls of Jericho are psychological this time, but they fall anyway. If the story of Bonnie Parker and Clyde Barrow seemed almost from the start, and even to them while they were living it, to be the material of legend, it's because robbers who are loyal to each other – like the James brothers – are a grade up from garden-variety robbers, and if they're male and female partners in crime and young and attractive they're a rare breed. The Barrow gang had both family loyalty and sex appeal working for their legend. David Newman and Robert Benton, who wrote the script for *Bonnie and Clyde*, were able to use the knowledge that, like many of our other famous outlaws and gangsters, the real Bonnie and Clyde seemed to others to be acting out forbidden roles and to relish their roles. In contrast with secret criminals – the furtive embezzlers and other crooks who lead seemingly honest lives – the known outlaws capture the public imagination, because they take chances, and because, often, they enjoy dramatizing their lives. They know that newspaper readers want all the details they can get about the criminals who do the terrible things they themselves don't dare to do, and also want the satisfaction of reading about the punishment after feasting on the crimes. Outlaws play to this public; they show off their big guns and fancy clothes and their defiance of the law. Bonnie and Clyde established the images for their own legend in the photographs they posed for: the gunman and the gun moll. The naïve, touching doggerel ballad that Bonnie Parker wrote and had published in newspapers is about the roles they play for other people contrasted with the coming end for them. It concludes:

> Someday they'll go down together;
> They'll bury them side by side;
> To few it'll be grief –
> To the law a relief –
> But it's death for Bonnie and Clyde.

That they did capture the public imagination is evidenced by the many movies based on their lives. In the late forties, there were *They Live by Night*, with Farley Granger and Cathy O'Donnell, and *Gun Crazy*, with John Dall and Peggy Cummins. (Alfred Hitchcock, in the same period, cast these two Clyde Barrows, Dall and Granger, as Loeb and Leopold, in *Rope*.) And there was a cheap – in every sense – 1958 exploitation film, *The Bonnie Parker Story*, starring Dorothy Provine. But the most important earlier version was Fritz Lang's *You Only Live Once*, starring Sylvia Sidney as "Joan" and Henry Fonda as "Eddie," which was made in 1937; this version, which was one of the best American films of the thirties, as *Bonnie and Clyde* is of the sixties, expressed certain feelings of its time, as this film expresses certain feelings of ours. (*They Live by Night*, produced by John Houseman under the aegis of Dore Schary, and directed by Nicholas Ray, was a very serious and socially significant tragic melodrama, but its attitudes were already dated thirties attitudes: the lovers were very young and pure and frightened and underprivileged; the hardened criminals were sordid; the settings were committedly grim. It made no impact on the postwar audience, though it was a great success in England, where our moldy socially significant movies could pass for courageous.)

Just how contemporary in feeling *Bonnie and Clyde* is may be indicated by contrasting it with *You Only Live Once*, which, though almost totally false to the historical facts, was *told* straight. It is a peculiarity of our times – perhaps it's one of the few specifically modern characteristics – that we don't take our stories straight any more. This isn't necessarily bad. *Bonnie and Clyde* is the first film demonstration that the put-on can be used for the purposes of art. *The Manchurian Candidate almost* succeeded in that, but what was implicitly wild and far-out in the material was nevertheless presented on screen as a straight thriller. *Bonnie and Clyde* keeps the audience in a kind of eager, nervous imbalance – holds our attention by throwing our disbelief back in our faces. To be put on is to be put on the spot, put on the stage, made the stooge in a comedy act. People in the audience at *Bonnie and Clyde* are laughing, demonstrating that they're not stooges – that they appreciate the joke – when they catch the first bullet right in the face. The movie keeps them off balance to the end. During the first part of the picture, a woman in my row was gleefully assuring her companions, "It's a comedy. It's a comedy." After a while, she didn't say anything. Instead of the movie spoof, which tells the audience that it doesn't need to feel or care, that it's all just in fun, that "we were only kidding," *Bonnie and Clyde* disrupts us with "And you thought we were only kidding."

This is the way the story was told in 1937. Eddie (Clyde) is a three-time loser who wants to work for a living, but nobody will give him a chance. Once you get on the wrong side of the law, "they" won't let you get back. Eddie knows it's hopeless – once a loser, always a loser. But his girl, Joan (Bonnie) – the only person who believes in him – thinks that an innocent man has nothing to fear. She marries him, and learns better. Arrested again and sentenced to death for a crime he didn't commit, Eddie asks her to smuggle a gun to him in prison, and she protests, "If I get you a gun, you'll kill somebody." He stares at her sullenly and asks, "What do you think they're going to do to me?" He becomes a murderer while escaping from prison; "society" has made him what it thought he was all along. *You Only Live Once* was an indictment of "society," of the forces of order that will not give Eddie the outcast a chance. "We have a right to live," Joan says as they set out across the country. During the time they are on the run, they become notorious outlaws; they are blamed for a series of crimes they didn't commit. (They do commit holdups, but only to get gas or groceries or medicine.) While the press pictures them as desperadoes robbing and killing and living high on the proceeds of crime, she is having a baby in a shack in a hobo jungle, and Eddie brings her a bouquet of wild flowers. Caught in a police trap, they die in each other's arms; they have been denied the right to live.

Because *You Only Live Once* was so well done, and because the audience in the thirties shared this view of the indifference and cruelty of "society," there were no protests against the sympathetic way the outlaws were pictured – and, indeed, there was no reason for any. In 1958, in *I Want to Live!* (a very popular, though not very good, movie), Barbara Graham, a drug-addict prostitute who had been executed for her share in the bludgeoning to death of an elderly woman, was presented as gallant, wronged, morally superior to everybody else in the movie, in order to strengthen the argument against capital punishment, and the director, Robert Wise, and his associates weren't accused of glorifying criminals, because the "criminals," as in *You Only Live Once*, weren't criminals but innocent victims. Why the protests, why are so many people upset (and not just the people who enjoy indignation), about *Bonnie and Clyde*, in which the criminals *are* criminals – Clyde an ignorant, sly near psychopath who thinks his crimes are accomplishments, and Bonnie a bored, restless waitress-slut who robs for excitement? And why so many accusations of historical inaccuracy, particularly against a work that is far more accurate historically than most and in which historical accuracy hardly matters anyway? There is always an issue of historical accuracy involved in any dramatic or literary work set in the past; indeed, it's fun to read about Richard III vs. Shakespeare's Richard III. The issue is always with us, and will always be with us as long as artists find stimulus in historical figures and want to present their versions of them. But why didn't movie critics attack, for example, *A Man for All Seasons* – which involves material of much more historical importance – for being historically inaccurate? Why attack *Bonnie and Clyde* more than the other movies based on the same pair, or more than the movie treatments of Jesse James or Billy the Kid or Dillinger or Capone or any of our other fictionalized outlaws? I would suggest that when a movie so clearly conceived as a new version of a legend is attacked as historically inaccurate, it's because it shakes people a little. I know this is based on some pretty sneaky psychological suppositions, but I don't see how else to account for the use only against a *good* movie of arguments that could be used against almost all movies. When I asked a nineteen-year-old boy who was raging against the movie as "a cliché-ridden fraud" if he got so worked up about other movies, he informed me that that was an argument *ad hominem*. And it is indeed. To ask why people react so angrily to the best movies and have so little negative reaction to poor ones is to imply that they are so unused to the experience of art in movies that they fight it.

Audiences at *Bonnie and Clyde* are not given a simple, secure basis for identification; they are made to feel but are not told *how* to feel. *Bonnie and Clyde* is not a serious melodrama involving us in the plight of the innocent but a movie that assumes – as William Wellman did in 1931 when he made *The Public Enemy*, with James Cagney as a smart, cocky, mean little crook – that we don't need to pretend we're interested only in the falsely accused, as if real criminals had no connection with us. There wouldn't be the popular excitement there is about outlaws if we didn't all suspect that – in some cases, at least – gangsters must take pleasure in the profits and glory of a life of crime. Outlaws wouldn't become legendary figures if we didn't suspect that there's more to crime than the social workers' case studies may show. And though what we've always been told will happen to them – that they'll come to a bad end – does seem to happen, some part of us wants to believe in the tiny possibility that they can get away with it. Is that really so terrible? Yet when it comes to movies people get nervous about acknowledging that there must be some fun in crime (though the gleam in Cagney's eye told its own story). *Bonnie and Clyde* shows the fun but uses it, too, making comedy out of the banality and conventionality of that fun. What looks ludicrous in this movie isn't *merely* ludicrous, and after we have laughed at ignorance and helplessness and emptiness and stupidity and idiotic deviltry, the laughs keep sticking in our throats, because what's funny isn't only funny.

In 1937, the movie-makers knew that the audience wanted to believe in the innocence of Joan and Eddie, because these two were lovers, and innocent lovers hunted down like animals made a tragic love story. In 1967, the movie-makers know that the audience wants to believe – maybe even prefers to believe – that Bonnie and Clyde were guilty of crimes, all right, but that they were innocent in general; that is, naïve and ignorant *compared with us*. The distancing of the sixties version shows the gangsters in an already legendary period, and part of what makes a legend for Americans is viewing anything that happened in the past as much simpler than what we are involved in now. We tend to find the past funny and the recent past campy-funny. The getaway cars of the early thirties are made to seem hilarious. (Imagine anyone getting away from a bank holdup in a tin lizzie like that!) In *You Only Live Once*, the outlaws existed in the same present as the audience, and there was (and still is, I'm sure) nothing funny about them; in *Bonnie and Clyde* that audience is in the movie, transformed into the poor people, the Depression people, of legend – with faces and poses out of Dorothea Lange and Walker Evans and *Let Us Now Praise Famous Men*. In 1937, the audience felt sympathy for the fugitives because they weren't allowed to lead normal lives; in 1967, the "normality" of the Barrow gang and their individual aspirations toward respectability are the craziest things about them – not just because they're killers but because thirties "normality" is in itself funny to us. The writers and the director of *Bonnie and Clyde* play upon our attitudes toward the American past by making the hats and guns and holdups look as dated as two-reel comedy; emphasizing the absurdity with banjo music, they make the period seem even farther away than it is. The Depression reminiscences are not used for purposes of social consciousness; hard times are not the reason for the Barrows' crimes, just the excuse. "We" didn't make Clyde a killer; the movie deliberately avoids easy sympathy by picking up Clyde when he is already a cheap crook. But Clyde is not the urban sharpster of *The Public Enemy*; he is the hick as bank robber – a countrified gangster, a hillbilly killer who doesn't mean any harm. People so simple that they are alienated from the results of their actions – like the primitives who don't connect babies with copulation – provide a kind of archetypal comedy for us. It may seem like a minor point that Bonnie and

Clyde are presented as not mean and sadistic, as having killed only when cornered; but in terms of legend, and particularly movie legend, it's a major one. The "classic" gangster films showed gang members betraying each other and viciously murdering the renegade who left to join another gang; the gang-leader hero no sooner got to the top than he was betrayed by someone he had trusted or someone he had double-crossed. In contrast, the Barrow gang represent family-style crime. And Newman and Benton have been acute in emphasizing this – not making them victims of society (they are never that, despite Penn's cloudy efforts along these lines) but making them absurdly "just-folks" ordi-nary. When Bonnie tells Clyde to pull off the road – "I want to talk to you" – they are in a getaway car, leaving the scene of a robbery, with the police right behind them, but they are absorbed in family bickering: the traditional all-American use of the family automobile. In a sense, it is the absence of sadism – it is the violence without sadism – that throws the audience off balance at *Bonnie and Clyde*. The brutality that comes out of this innocence is far more shocking than the calculated brutalities of mean killers.

Playfully posing with their guns, the real Bonnie and Clyde mocked the "Bloody Barrows" of the Hearst press. One photograph shows slim, pretty Bonnie, smiling and impeccably dressed, pointing a huge gun at Clyde's chest as he, a dimpled dude with a cigar, smiles back. The famous picture of Bonnie in the same clothes but looking ugly squinting into the sun, with a foot on the car, a gun on her hip, and a cigar in her mouth, is obviously a joke – her caricature of herself as a gun moll. Probably, since they never meant to kill, they thought the "Bloody Barrows" were a joke – a creation of the lying newspapers.

There's something new working for the Bonnie-and-Clyde legend now: our nostalgia for the thirties – the unpredictable, contrary affec-tion of the prosperous for poverty, or at least for the artifacts, the tokens, of poverty, for Pop culture seen in the dreariest rural settings, where it truly seems to belong. Did people in the cities listen to the Eddie Cantor show? No doubt they did, but the sound of his voice, like the sound of Ed Sullivan now, evokes a primordial, pre-urban existence – the childhood of the race. Our comic-melancholic affection for thirties Pop has become sixties Pop, and those who made *Bonnie and Clyde* are smart enough to use it that way. Being knowing is not an artist's highest gift, but it can make a hell of a lot of difference in a movie. In the

American experience, the miseries of the Depression are funny in the way that the Army is funny to draftees – a shared catastrophe, a leveling, forming part of our common background. Those too young to remember the Depression have heard about it from their parents. (When I was at college, we used to top each other's stories about how our families had survived: the fathers who had committed suicide so that their wives and children could live off the insurance; the mothers trying to make a game out of the meals of potatoes cooked on an open fire.) Though the American derision of the past has many offensive aspects, it has some good ones, too, because it's a way of making fun not only of our forebears but of ourselves and our pretensions. The toughness about what we've come out of and what we've been through – the honesty to see ourselves as the Yahoo children of yokels – is a good part of American popular art. There is a kind of American poetry in a stickup gang seen chasing across the bedraggled backdrop of the Depression (as true in its way as Nabokov's vision of Humbert Humbert and Lolita in the cross-country world of motels) – as if crime were the only activity in a country stupefied by poverty. But Arthur Penn doesn't quite have the toughness of mind to know it; it's not what he means by poetry. His squatters'-jungle scene is too "eloquent," like a poster making an appeal, and the Parker-family-reunion sequence is poetic in the gauzy mode. He makes the sequence a fancy lyric interlude, like a number in a musical (*Funny Face*, to be exact); it's too "imaginative" – a literal dust bowl, as thoroughly becalmed as Sleeping Beauty's garden. The movie becomes dreamy-soft where it should be hard (and hard-edged).

If there is such a thing as an American tragedy, it must be funny. O'Neill undoubtedly felt this when he had James Tyrone get up to turn off the lights in *Long Day's Journey Into Night*. We are bumpkins, haunted by the bottle of ketchup on the dining table at San Simeon. We garble our foreign words and phrases and hope that at least we've used them right. Our heroes pick up the wrong fork, and the basic figure of fun in the American theatre and American movies is the man who puts on airs. Children of peddlers and hod carriers don't feel at home in tragedy; we are used to failure. But, because of the quality of American life at the present time, perhaps there can be no real comedy – nothing more than stupidity and "spoof" – without true horror in it. Bonnie and Clyde and their partners in crime are comically bad bank robbers, and the backdrop of poverty makes their holdups seem pathetically tacky, yet they rob banks and kill people; Clyde and his good-natured brother are so shallow they never think much about anything, yet they suffer and die.

If this way of holding more than one attitude toward life is already familiar to us – if we recognize the make-believe robbers whose toy guns produce real blood, and the Keystone cops who shoot them dead, from Truffaut's *Shoot the Piano Player* and Godard's gangster pictures, *Breathless* and *Band of Outsiders* – it's because the young French directors discovered the poetry of crime in American life (from our movies) and showed the Americans how to put it on the screen in a new, "existential" way. Melodramas and gangster movies and comedies were always more our speed than "prestigious," "distinguished" pictures; the French directors who grew up on American pictures found poetry in our fast action, laconic speech, plain gestures. And because they understood that you don't express your love of life by denying the comedy or the horror of it, they brought out the poetry in our tawdry subjects. Now Arthur Penn, working with a script heavily influenced – one might almost say inspired – by Truffaut's *Shoot the Piano Player*, unfortunately imitates Truffaut's artistry instead of going back to its tough American sources. The French may tenderize their American material, but we shouldn't. That turns into another way of making "prestigious," "distinguished" pictures.

Probably part of the discomfort that people feel about *Bonnie and Clyde* grows out of its compromises and its failures. I wish the script hadn't provided the upbeat of the hero's sexual success as a kind of sop to the audience. I think what makes us not believe in it is that it isn't consistent with the intelligence of the rest of the writing – that it isn't on the same level, because it's too manipulatively clever, too much of a gimmick. (The scene that shows the gnomish gang member called C. W. sleeping in the same room with Bonnie and Clyde suggests other possibilities, perhaps discarded, as does C. W.'s reference to Bonnie's liking his tattoo.) Compromises are not new to the Bonnie-and-Clyde story; *You Only Live Once* had a tacked-on coda featuring a Heavenly choir and William Gargan as a dead priest, patronizing Eddie even in the afterlife, welcoming him to Heaven with "You're free, Eddie!" The kind of people who make a movie like *You Only Live Once* are not the kind who write endings like that, and, by the same sort of internal evidence, I'd guess that Newman and Benton, whose Bonnie seems to owe so much to

Catherine in *Jules and Jim*, had more interesting ideas originally about Bonnie's and Clyde's (and maybe C. W.'s) sex lives.

But people also feel uncomfortable about the violence, and here I think they're wrong. That is to say, they *should* feel uncomfortable, but this isn't an argument *against* the movie. Only a few years ago, a good director would have suggested the violence obliquely, with reaction shots (like the famous one in *The Golden Coach*, when we see a whole bullfight reflected in Anna Magnani's face), and death might have been symbolized by a light going out, or stylized, with blood and wounds kept to a minimum. In many ways, this method is more effective; we feel the violence more because so much is left to our imaginations. But the whole point of *Bonnie and Clyde* is to rub our noses in it, to make us pay our dues for laughing. The dirty reality of death – not suggestions but blood and holes – is necessary. Though I generally respect a director's skill and intelligence in inverse ratio to the violence he shows on the screen, and though I questioned even the Annie Sullivan–Helen Keller fight scenes in Arthur Penn's *The Miracle Worker*, I think that this time Penn is right. (I think he was also right when he showed violence in his first film, *The Left Handed Gun*, in 1958.) Suddenly, in the last few years, our view of the world has gone beyond "good taste." Tasteful suggestions of violence would at this point be a more grotesque form of comedy than *Bonnie and Clyde* attempts. *Bonnie and Clyde* needs violence; violence is its meaning. When, during a comically botched-up getaway, a man is shot in the face, the image is obviously based on one of the most famous sequences in Eisenstein's *Potemkin* – to convey in an instant how someone who just happens to be in the wrong place at the wrong time, the irrelevant "innocent" bystander, can get it full in the face. And at that instant the meaning of Clyde Barrow's character changes; he's still a clown, but *we've* become the butt of the joke.

It is a kind of violence that says something to us; it is something that movies must be free to use. And it is just because artists must be free to use violence – a legal right that is beginning to come under attack – that we must also defend the legal rights of those film-makers who use violence to sell tickets, for it is not the province of the law to decide that one man is an artist and another man a no-talent. The no-talent has as much right to produce works as the artist has, and not only because he has a surprising way of shifting from one category to the other but also because men have an inalienable right to be untalented, and the law should not discriminate against lousy "artists." I am not saying that the violence in *Bonnie and Clyde* is legally acceptable because the film is a work of art; I think that *Bonnie and Clyde*, though flawed, is a work of art, but I think that the violence in *The Dirty Dozen*, which isn't a work of art, and whose violence offends me *personally*, should also be legally defensible, however morally questionable. Too many people – including some movie reviewers – want the law to take over the job of movie criticism; perhaps what they really want is for their own criticisms to have the force of law. Such people see *Bonnie and Clyde* as a danger to public morality; they think an audience goes to a play or a movie and takes the actions in it as examples for imitation. They look at the world and blame the movies. But if women who are angry with their husbands take it out on the kids, I don't think we can blame *Medea* for it; if, as has been said, we are a nation of mother-lovers, I don't think we can place the blame on *Oedipus Rex*. Part of the power of art lies in showing us what we are *not* capable of. We see that killers are not a different breed but are *us* without the insight or understanding or self-control that works of art strengthen. The tragedy of *Macbeth* is in the fall from nobility to horror; the comic tragedy of *Bonnie and Clyde* is that although you can't fall from the bottom you can reach the same horror. The movies may set styles in dress- or love-making, they may advertise cars or beverages, but art is not examples for imitation – that is not what a work of art does for us – though that is what guardians of morality *think* art is and what they want it to be and why they think a good movie is one that sets "healthy," "cheerful" examples of behavior, like a giant all-purpose commercial for the American way of life. But people don't "buy" what they see in a movie quite so simply; Louis B. Mayer did not turn us into a nation of Andy Hardys, and if, in a film, we see a frightened man wantonly take the life of another, it does not encourage us to do the same, any more than seeing an ivory hunter shoot an elephant makes us want to shoot one. It may, on the contrary, so sensitize us that we get a pang in the gut if we accidentally step on a moth.

Will we, as some people have suggested, be lured into imitating the violent crimes of Clyde and Bonnie because Warren Beatty and Faye Dunaway are "glamorous"? Do they, as some people have charged, confer glamour on violence? It's difficult to see how, since the characters they play are horrified by it and ultimately destroyed by it. Nobody in the movie gets pleasure from violence. Is the charge based on the notion that simply by their presence in the movie Warren Beatty and Faye Dunaway make crime attractive? If movie stars can't play criminals without our all wanting to be criminals, then maybe the only safe roles for them to play are movie stars – which, in this assumption, everybody wants to be anyway. After all, if they played factory workers, the economy might be dislocated by everybody's trying to become a factory worker. (Would having criminals played by dwarfs or fatties discourage crime? It seems rather doubtful.) The accusation that the beauty of movie stars makes the anti-social acts of their characters dangerously attractive is the kind of contrived argument we get from people who are bothered by something and are clutching at straws. Actors and actresses are *usually* more beautiful than ordinary people. And why not? Garbo's beauty notwithstanding, her Anna Christie did not turn us into whores, her Mata Hari did not turn us into spies, her Anna Karenina did not make us suicides. We did not want her to be ordinary looking. Why should we be deprived of the pleasure of beauty? Garbo could be all women in love because, being more beautiful than life, she could more beautifully express emotions. It is a supreme asset for actors and actresses to be beautiful; it gives them greater range and greater possibilities for expressiveness. The handsomer they are, the more roles they can play; Olivier can be anything, but who would want to see Ralph Richardson, great as he is, play Antony? Actors and actresses who are beautiful start with an enormous advantage, because we love to look at them. The joke in the glamour charge is that Faye Dunaway has the magazine-illustration look of countless uninterestingly pretty girls, and Warren Beatty has the kind of high-school good looks that are generally lost fast. It's the roles that make *them* seem glamorous. Good roles do that for actors.

There is a story told against Beatty in a recent *Esquire* – how during the shooting of *Lilith* he "delayed a scene for three days demanding the line 'I've read *Crime and Punishment* and *The Brothers Karamazov*' be changed to 'I've read *Crime and Punishment* and half of *The Brothers Karamazov*.'" Considerations of professional conduct aside, what is odd is why his adversaries waited three days to give in, because, of course, he was right. That's what the character he played *should* say; the other way, the line has no point at all. But this kind of intuition isn't enough to make an actor, and in a number of roles Beatty, probably because he doesn't have the technique to make the most of his lines in the least possible time, has depended too much on intuitive non-acting – holding the screen far too long as he acted out self-preoccupied characters in a lifelike, boringly self-conscious way. He has a gift for slyness, though, as he showed in *The Roman Spring of Mrs. Stone*, and in most of his films he could hold the screen – maybe because there seemed to be something going on in his mind, some kind of calculation. There was something smart about him – something shrewdly private in juvenile roles. Beatty was the producer of *Bonnie and Clyde*, responsible for keeping the company on schedule, and he has been quoted as saying, "There's not a scene that we have done that we couldn't do better by taking another day." This is the hell of the expensive way of making movies, but it probably helps to explain why Beatty is more intense than he has been before and why he has picked up his pace. His business sense may have improved his timing. The role of Clyde Barrow seems to have released something in him. As Clyde, Beatty is good with his eyes and mouth and his hat, but his body is still inexpressive; he doesn't have a trained actor's use of his body, and watching him move, one is never for a minute convinced he's impotent. It is, however, a tribute to his performance that one singles this failure out. His slow timing works perfectly in the sequence in which he offers the dispossessed farmer his gun; there may not be another actor who would have dared to prolong the scene that way, and the prolongation until the final "We rob banks" gives the sequence its comic force. I have suggested elsewhere that one of the reasons that rules are impossible in the arts is that in movies (and in the other arts, too) the new "genius" – the genuine as well as the fraudulent or the dubious – is often the man who has enough audacity, or is simpleminded enough, to do what others had the good taste not to do. Actors before Brando did not mumble and scratch and show their sweat; dramatists before Tennessee Williams did not make explicit a particular substratum of American erotic fantasy; movie directors before Orson Welles did not dramatize the techniques of film-making; directors before Richard Lester did not lay out the whole movie as cleverly as the opening credits; actresses before Marilyn Monroe did not make an asset of their ineptitude by turning faltering misreadings into an appealing style. Each, in a large way, did something that people had always enjoyed and were often embarrassed or ashamed about enjoying. Their "bad taste" shaped a new accepted taste. Beatty's non-actor's "bad" timing may be this kind of "genius"; we seem to be watching him *think out* his next move.

It's difficult to know how Bonnie should have been played, because the character isn't worked out. Here the script seems weak. She is made too warmly sympathetic – and sympathetic in a style that antedates the style of the movie. Being frustrated and moody, she's not funny enough – neither ordinary, which, in the circumstances, would be comic, nor perverse, which might be rather funny, too. Her attitude toward her mother is too loving. There could be something funny about her wanting to run home to her mama, but, as it has been done, her heading home, running off through the fields, is unconvincing – incompletely motivated. And because the element of the ridiculous that makes the others so individual has been left out of her character she doesn't seem to belong to the period as the others do. Faye Dunaway has a sixties look anyway – not just because her eyes are made up in a sixties way and her hair is wrong but because her personal style and her acting are sixties. (This may help to make her popular; she can seem prettier to those who don't recognize prettiness except in the latest styles.) Furthermore, in some difficult-to-define way, Faye Dunaway as Bonnie doesn't keep her distance – that is to say, an *actor's* distance – either from the role or from the audience. She doesn't hold a characterization; she's in and out of emotions all the time, and though she often hits effective ones, the emotions seem *hers*, not the character's. She has some talent, but she comes on too strong; she makes one conscious that she's a willing worker, but she doesn't seem to know what she's doing – rather like Bonnie in her attempts to overcome Clyde's sexual difficulties.

Although many daily movie reviewers judge a movie in isolation, as if the people who made it had no previous history, more serious critics now commonly attempt to judge a movie as an expressive vehicle of the director, and a working out of his personal themes. Auden has written, "Our judgment of an established author is never simply an aesthetic judgment. In addition to any literary merit it may have, a new book by him has a historic interest for us as the act of a person in whom we have long been interested. He is not only a poet . . . he is also a character in our biography." For a while, people went to the newest Bergman and the newest Fellini that way; these movies were greeted like the latest novels of a favorite author. But Arthur Penn is not a writer-director like Bergman or Fellini, both of whom began as writers, and who (even though Fellini employs several collaborators) compose their spiritual autobiographies step by step on film. Penn is far more dependent on the talents of others, and his primary material – what he starts with – does not come out of his own experience. If the popular audience is generally uninterested in the director (unless he is heavily publicized, like De Mille or Hitchcock), the audience that is interested in the art of movies has begun, with many of the critics, to think of movies as a directors' medium to the point where they tend to ignore the contribution of the writers – and the directors may be almost obscenely content to omit mention of the writers. The history of the movies is being rewritten to disregard facts in favor of celebrating the director as the sole "creative" force. One can read Josef von Sternberg's autobiography and the text of the latest books on his movies without ever finding the name of Jules Furthman, the writer who worked on nine of his most famous movies (including *Morocco* and *Shanghai Express*). Yet the appearance of Furthman's name in the credits of such Howard Hawks films as *Only Angels Have Wings, To Have and Have Not, The Big Sleep*, and *Rio Bravo* suggests the reason for the similar qualities of good-bad-girl glamour in the roles played by Dietrich and Bacall and in other von Sternberg and Hawks heroines, and also in the Jean Harlow and Constance Bennett roles in the movies he wrote for *them*. Furthman, who has written about half of the most entertaining movies to come out of Hollywood (Ben Hecht wrote most of the other half), isn't even listed in new encyclopedias of the film. David Newman and Robert Benton may be good enough to join this category of unmentionable men who do what the directors are glorified for. The Hollywood writer is becoming a ghostwriter. The writers who succeed in the struggle to protect their identity and their material by becoming writer-directors or writer-producers soon become too rich and powerful to bother doing their own writing. And they rarely have the visual sense or the training to make good movie directors.

Anyone who goes to big American movies like *Grand Prix* and *The Sand Pebbles* recognizes that movies with scripts like those don't have a chance to be anything more than exercises in technology, and that this is what is meant by the decadence of American movies. In the past, directors used to say that they were no better than their material. (Sometimes they said it when they weren't even up to their material.) A good director can attempt to camouflage poor writing with craftsmanship and style, but ultimately no amount of director's skill can conceal a writer's failure; a poor script, even well directed, results in a stupid movie – as, unfortunately, does a good script poorly directed. Despite the new notion that the direction is everything, Penn can't redeem bad material, nor, as one may surmise from his *Mickey One*, does he necessarily know when it's bad. It is not fair to judge Penn by a film like *The Chase*, because he evidently did not have artistic control over the production, but what happens when he does have control and is working with a poor, pretentious mess of a script is painfully apparent in *Mickey One* – an art film in the worst sense of that term. Though one cannot say of *Bonnie and Clyde* to what degree it shows the work of Newman and Benton and to what degree they merely enabled Penn to "express himself," there are ways of making guesses. As we hear the lines, we can detect the intentions even when the intentions are not quite carried out. Penn is a little clumsy and rather too fancy; he's too much interested in being cinematically creative and artistic to know when to trust the script. *Bonnie and Clyde* could be better if it were simpler. Nevertheless, Penn is a remarkable director when he has something to work with. His most interesting previous work was in his first film, *The Left Handed Gun* (and a few bits of *The Miracle Worker*, a good movie version of the William Gibson play, which he had also directed on the stage and on television). *The Left Handed Gun*, with Paul Newman as an ignorant Billy the Kid in the sex-starved, male-dominated Old West, has the same kind of violent, legendary, nostalgic material as *Bonnie and Clyde*; its script, a rather startling one, was adapted by Leslie Stevens from a Gore Vidal television play. In interviews, Penn makes high, dull sounds – more like a politician than a movie director. But he has a gift for violence, and, despite all the violence in movies, a gift for it is rare. (Eisenstein had it, and Dovzhenko, and Buñuel, but not many others.) There are few memorable violent moments in American movies, but there is one in Penn's first film: Billy's shotgun blasts a man right out of one of his boots; the man falls in the street, but his boot remains upright; a little girl's giggle at the boot is interrupted by her mother's slapping her. The mother's slap – the seal of the awareness of horror – says that even children must learn that some things that look funny are not only funny. That slap, saying that only idiots would laugh at pain and death, that a child must develop sensibility, is the same slap that *Bonnie and Clyde* delivers to the woman saying "It's a comedy." In *The Left Handed Gun*, the slap is itself funny, and yet we suck in our breath; we do not dare to laugh.

Some of the best American movies show the seams of cuts and the confusions of compromises and still hold together, because there is enough energy and spirit to carry the audience over each of the weak episodes to the next good one. The solid intelligence of the writing and Penn's aura of sensitivity help *Bonnie and Clyde* triumph over many poorly directed scenes: Bonnie posing for the photograph with the Texas Ranger, or – the worst sequence – the Ranger getting information out of Blanche Barrow in the hospital. The attempt to make the Texas Ranger an old-time villain doesn't work. He's in the tradition of the mustachioed heavy who foreclosed mortgages and pursued heroines in turn-of-the-century plays, and this one-dimensional villainy belongs, glaringly, to spoof. In some cases, I think, the writing and the conception of the scenes are better (potentially, that is) than the way the scenes have been directed and acted. If Gene Hackman's Buck Barrow is a beautifully controlled performance, the best in the film, several of the other players – though they are very good – needed a tighter rein. They act too much. But it is in other ways that Penn's limitations show – in his excessive reliance on meaning-laden closeups, for one. And it's no wonder he wasn't able to bring out the character of Bonnie in scenes like the one showing her appreciation of the fingernails on the figurine, for in other scenes his own sense of beauty appears to be only a few rungs farther up that same cultural ladder.

The showpiece sequence, Bonnie's visit to her mother (which is a bit reminiscent of Humphrey Bogart's confrontation with his mother, Marjorie Main, in the movie version of *Dead End*), aims for an effect of alienation, but that effect is confused by all the other things attempted in the sequence: the poetic echoes of childhood (which also echo the child sliding down the hill in *Jules and Jim*) and a general attempt to create a frieze from our national past – a poetry of poverty. Penn isn't quite up to it, though he is at least good enough to communicate what he is trying to do, and it is an attempt that one can respect. In 1939, John Ford attempted a similar poetic evocation of the legendary American past in *Young Mr. Lincoln*; this kind of evocation, by getting at how we *feel* about the past, moves us far more than attempts at historical re-creation. When Ford's Western evocations fail, they become languorous; when they succeed, they are the West of our dreams, and his Lincoln, the man so humane and so smart that he can outwit the unjust and save the innocent, is the Lincoln of our dreams, as the Depression of *Bonnie and Clyde* is the Depression of our dreams – the nation in a kind of trance, as in a dim memory. In this sense, the effect of blur is justified, is "right." Our memories *have* become hazy; this is what the Depression has faded into. But we are too conscious of the technical means used to achieve this blur, of the *attempt* at poetry. We are aware that the filtered effects already include our responses, and it's too easy; the lines are good enough so that the stylization wouldn't have been necessary if the scene had been played right. A simple frozen frame might have been more appropriate.

The editing of this movie is, however, the best editing in an American movie in a long time, and one may assume that Penn deserves credit for it along with the editor, Dede Allen. It's particularly inventive in the robberies and in the comedy sequence of Blanche running through the police barricades with her kitchen spatula in her hand. (There is, however, one bad bit of editing: the end of the hospital scene, when Blanche's voice makes an emotional shift without a corresponding change in her facial position.) The quick panic of Bonnie and Clyde looking at each other's face for the last time is a stunning example of the art of editing.

The end of the picture, the rag-doll dance of death as the gun blasts keep the bodies of Bonnie and Clyde in motion, is brilliant. It is a horror that seems to go on for eternity, and yet it doesn't last a second beyond what it should. The audience leaving the theatre is the quietest audience imaginable.

Still, that woman near me was saying "It's a comedy" for a little too long, and although this could have been, and probably was, a demonstration of plain old-fashioned insensitivity, it suggests that those who have attuned themselves to the "total" comedy of the last few years may not know when to stop laughing. Movie audiences have been getting a steady diet of "black" comedy since 1964 and *Dr. Strangelove, Or: How I Learned to Stop Worrying and Love the Bomb*. Spoof and satire have been entertaining audiences since the two-reelers; because it is so easy to do on film things that are difficult or impossible in nature, movies are ideally suited to exaggerations of heroic prowess and to the kind of lighthearted nonsense we used to get when even the newsreels couldn't resist the kidding finish of the speeded-up athletic competition or the diver flying up from the water. The targets have usually been social and political fads and abuses, together with the heroes and the clichés of the just preceding period of film-making. *Dr. Strangelove* opened a new movie era. It ridiculed *everything* and *everybody* it showed, but concealed its own liberal pieties, thus protecting itself from ridicule. A professor who had told me that *The Manchurian Candidate* was "irresponsible," adding, "I didn't like it – I can suspend disbelief only so far," was overwhelmed by *Dr. Strangelove*: "I've never been so involved. I had to keep reminding myself it was only a movie." *Dr. Strangelove* was clearly intended as a cautionary movie; it meant to jolt us awake to the dangers of the bomb by showing us the insanity of the course we were pursuing. But artists' warnings about war and the dangers of total annihilation never tell us how we are supposed to regain control, and *Dr. Strangelove*, chortling over madness, did not indicate any possibilities for sanity. It was experienced not as satire but as a confirmation of fears. Total laughter carried the day. A new generation enjoyed seeing the world as insane; they *literally* learned to stop worrying and love the bomb. Conceptually, we had already been living with the bomb; now the mass audience of the movies – which is the youth of America – grasped the idea that the threat of extinction can be used to devaluate everything, to turn it all into a joke. And the members of this audience do love the bomb; they love feeling that the worst has happened and the irrational are the sane, because there is the bomb as the proof that the rational are insane. They love the bomb because it intensifies their feelings of hopelessness and powerlessness and innocence. It's only three years since Lewis Mumford was widely acclaimed for saying about *Dr. Strangelove* that "unless the spectator was purged by laughter he would be paralyzed by the unendurable anxiety this policy, once it were honestly appraised, would produce." Far from being purged, the spectators are paralyzed, but they're still laughing. And how odd it is now to read, "*Dr. Strangelove* would be a silly, ineffective picture if its purpose were to ridicule the characters of our military and political leaders by showing them as clownish monsters – stupid, psychotic, obsessed." From *Dr. Strangelove* it's a quick leap to *MacBird* and to a belief in exactly what it was said we weren't meant to find in *Dr. Strangelove*. It is not war that has been laughed to scorn but the possibility of sane action.

Once something enters mass culture, it travels fast. In the spoofs of the last few years, everything is gross, ridiculous, insane; to make sense would be to risk being square. This is the context in which *Bonnie and Clyde*, an entertaining movie that has some feeling in it, upsets people – people who didn't get upset even by *Mondo Cane*. Maybe it's because *Bonnie and Clyde*, by making us care about the robber lovers, has put the sting back into death.

Filmography

Although this book concerns mainly the films of Arthur Penn, particularly *Bonnie and Clyde*, it is important to note that Penn began his long and diverse career in live television, directing for such prestigious programs as the *Colgate Comedy Hour* (1951–3), *Gulf Playhouse: First Person* (1953), *Philco-Goodyear Playhouse* (1954), *Producer's Showcase* (1954), and *Playhouse 90* (1957–8).

Because of his extensive experience in live television production, Penn was asked to serve as advisor to John F. Kennedy during the famous Kennedy-Nixon Presidential Debates. He ultimately directed the third of these historic television debates.

Penn has also had an illustrious stage career on Broadway, where he directed plays such as *Blue Denim* (1955), *Two for the Seesaw* (1958), *The Miracle Worker* (1959), *Toys in the Attic* (1960), *An Evening with Mike Nichols and Elaine May* (1960), *All the Way Home* (1960), *Golden Boy . . . The Musical* (1964), *Wait Until Dark* (1966), *Sly Fox* (1976), and *Golda* (1977).

The following films were directed by Arthur Penn:

1958

The Left-Handed Gun
Producer: Fred Coe
Screenplay: Leslie Stevens (based on Gore Vidal's play, *The Death of Billy the Kid*)
Cast: Paul Newman, John Dehner, Hurd Hatfield, Lita Milan

1962

The Miracle Worker
Producer: Fred Coe
Screenplay: William Gibson (from his Broadway play)
Cast: Anne Bancroft, Patty Duke, Victor Jory, Inga Swenson, Andrew Prine

1964

Mickey One
Producer: Arthur Penn
Screenplay: Alan Surgal
Cast: Warren Beatty, Alexandra Stewart, Hurd Hatfield, Franchot Tone, Jeff Corey

1966

The Chase
Producer: Sam Spiegel
Screenplay: Lillian Hellman (based on Horton Foote's play, *The Chase*)
Cast: Marlon Brando, Jane Fonda, Robert Redford, E. G. Marshall, Angie Dickinson, Janice Rule, Robert Duvall, James Fox

1967

Bonnie and Clyde
Producer: Warren Beatty
Screenplay: David Newman and Robert Benton
Cast: Warren Beatty, Faye Dunaway, Michael J. Pollard, Gene Hackman, Estelle Parsons, Denver Pyle, Dub Taylor, Evans Evans, Gene Wilder

1969

Alice's Restaurant
Producer: Hillard Elkins, Joe Manduke
Screenplay: Venable Herndon, Arthur Penn (based on Arlo Guthrie's song, "The Alice's Restaurant Massacre")
Cast: Arlo Guthrie, Pat Quinn, James Broderick, Michael McClanathan

1970

Little Big Man
Producer: Stuart Millar, Arthur Penn
Screenplay: Calder Willingham (from Thomas Berger's novel, *Little Big Man*)
Cast: Dustin Hoffman, Faye Dunaway, Martin Balsam, Richard Mulligan, Chief Dan George

1973

Visions of Eight ("The Highest")
Producer: Stuart Margulies

1975

Night Moves
Producer: Robert M. Sherman
Screenplay: Alan Sharp (based on his novel, *Night Moves*)
Cast: Gene Hackman, Susan Clark, Jennifer Warren, James Woods, Melanie Griffith

1976

The Missouri Breaks
Producer: Elliott Kastner, Robert M. Sherman
Screenplay: Thomas McGuane
Cast: Marlon Brando, Jack Nicholson, Randy Quaid, Kathleen Lloyd, Frederic Forrest

1981

Four Friends
Producer: Gene Lasko, Arthur Penn
Screenplay: Steve Teisch

Cast: Craig Wasson, Jodi Thelen, Michael Huddleston, Jim Metzler, Reed Birney

1985

Target
Producer: Richard D. Zanuck, David Brown
Screenplay: Howard Berk, Don Peterson
Cast: Gene Hackman, Matt Dillon, Gayle Hunnicutt, Josef Summer, Ilona Grubel

1986

Dead of Winter
Producer: John Bloomgarden, Marc Shmuger
Screenplay: Marc Shmuger, Mark Malone
Cast: Mary Steenburgen, Roddy McDowall, Jan Rubes, William Russ

1988

Penn and Teller Get Killed
Producer: Arthur Penn
Screenplay: Penn Jillette, Teller
Cast: Penn Jillette, Teller

1992

The Portrait
Producer: Robert Greenwald, Gregory Peck, Carla Singer
Screenplay: Tina Howard, Lynn Roth (from Howard's play, *Painting Churches*)
Cast: Gregory Peck, Lauren Bacall, Cecilia Peck

1995

Inside
Producer: Hillard Elkins
Screenplay: Bima Stagg
Cast: Nigel Hawthorne, Eric Stoltz, Louis Gossett, Jr., Ian Roberts

Select Bibliography

Cawelti, John G., ed. *Focus on "Bonnie and Clyde."* Englewood Cliffs, NJ: Prentice-Hall, 1973.

Cott, Nancy F. "Bonnie and Clyde." In *Past Imperfect: History According to the Movies*, edited by Mark C. Carnes, 220–3. New York: Henry Holt and Co., 1995.

Giannetti, Louis. *Masters of the Modern Cinema.* Englewood Cliffs, NJ: Prentice-Hall, 1981.

Kolker, Robert Phillip. *A Cinema of Loneliness: Penn, Kubrick, Scorsese, Spielberg, Altman.* 2d ed. New York: Oxford University Press, 1988.

Mahoney, Edward George. *Penn's Woods: America in the Films of Arthur Penn.* Ann Arbor, MI: University Microfilms International, 1985.

Man, Glenn. *Radical Visions: American Film Renaissance, 1967–1976.* Contribution to the Study of Popular Culture 41. Westport, CT: Greenwood Press, 1994.

Muray, Edward. *Ten Film Classics: A Re-Viewing.* New York: Frederick Ungar Publishing Co., 1978.

Shadoian, Jack. *Dreams and Dead Ends: The American Gangster/Crime Film.* Cambridge, MA: The MIT Press, 1979.

Thomas, Sam, ed. *Best American Screenplays.* New York: Crown Publishers, 1986.

Toplin, Robert Brent. *History by Hollywood: The Uses and Abuses of the American Past.* Urbana, IL: The University of Illinois Press, 1996.

Wake, Sandra, and Nicola Hayden, comps. and eds. *Bonnie and Clyde.*

New York: Lorrimer Publishing, 1972; reprint, Surrey, England, 1983.

Wood, Robin. *Arthur Penn*. New York: Frederick A. Praeger, 1969.

Zuker, Joel S. *Arthur Penn: A Guide to References and Resources*. Boston: G. K. Hall and Co., 1980.

Index